Beyond the Ego

Where Love, Joy, and Peace of Mind Await You

David Mutchler

BALBOA.
PRESS

A DIVISION OF HAY HOUSE

ISBN: 978-1-4525-4468-7 (e)
ISBN: 978-1-4525-4469-4 (sc)
ISBN: 978-1-4525-4470-0 (hc)
Library of Congress Control Number: 2011963547

Balboa Press books may be ordered through booksellers or by contacting:

Balboa Press
A Division of Hay House
1663 Liberty Drive
Bloomington, IN 47403
www.balboapress.com
1-(877) 407-4847

Because of the dynamic nature of the Internet, any web addresses or
links contained in this book may have changed since publication and
may no longer be valid. The views expressed in this work are solely those
of the author and do not necessarily reflect the views of the publisher,
and the publisher hereby disclaims any responsibility for them.

The author of this book does not dispense medical advice or prescribe the use
of any technique as a form of treatment for physical, emotional, or medical
problems without the advice of a physician, either directly or indirectly. The
intent of the author is only to offer information of a general nature to help you
in your quest for emotional and spiritual well-being. In the event you use any
of the information in this book for yourself, which is your constitutional right,
the author and the publisher assume no responsibility for your actions.

Any people depicted in stock imagery provided by Thinkstock are models,
and such images are being used for illustrative purposes only.
Certain stock imagery © Thinkstock.

Printed in the United States of America
Balboa Press rev. date: 1/23/2012

Table of Contents

Part VI: Spirit Has a Language of Its Own

Part VII: Conclusion

Preface

Spirit moved and the book was conceived.
From whence it cometh and wither it goeth,
Spirit alone can know.
Known is that ego is
complex and mysterious,
troublemaking and subtle,
pain-seeking and powerful,
yet *powerless* to the touch of Spirit
which quiets the storm.
What draws one to Spirit's light?
Readiness and nothing more.
When the student is ready,
the teacher will appear.

David Mutchler
Grand Rapids, Michigan

Part I

Introduction
and
Overview

Chapter One

INTRODUCTION

I was in a health food store recently and couldn't help but overhear one of the owners speaking loudly to a customer. For the moment at least, he was so passionate in his views about the state of the world that the tone of his voice apparently didn't much matter to him. While I missed the beginning of his argument, it would have been difficult to not hear the conclusion, and I quote: "Let's face it; the world is on the edge of going stark raving mad!"

Though he was surely not the first or last person to argue this point, one has to admit that perhaps this man, as much now as ever before, has a defensible position. As best I could decipher, his specific concern was that due to the mass production of our food supply, our bodies are being systematically depleted of essential nutrients; that over time this will have increasingly serious repercussions on our health and well-being; and that most of the popular remedies are medical and pharmaceutical in nature and tend to address the symptoms of the problem rather than focus on the root cause, which is nutritional deficiency.

Admittedly, this man's conclusion as to the state of the world was based on a single slice of a much larger pie. Yet one need not look far to conclude that the world is faced with a number of serious challenges. At this time we are in a global recession. Millions of people are losing their jobs, their homes, their health care benefits, their retirement funds, their patience, and, in many cases, their hope. Corporate executives are walking off with multimillion-dollar bonuses while those they employ go into retirement penniless due to misguided management driven by greed. The United States is now fighting its second war against rogue nations, which are ruled by leaders with value systems vastly opposed to our own and who work feverishly to destroy us.

History would say that this too shall pass, which it may well do. Yet rising numbers of people are anxious that even if all these things are fixed, our lives will nonetheless never be quite the same. We are fast becoming a world economy, and the reality is that globalization is here to stay. Periodic economic events in recent times have demonstrated all too clearly that one significant slipup by any one of a growing number of nations can, in a flash, shift the whole world out of balance. When this happens, it gives pause for concern as to what exactly the future may hold in store. And while this question used to be a matter more of national importance, it now has international significance that begs for rapid, yet sound solutions.

In addition to the angst that world tensions spawn, we need only look as far as our own living rooms to be frightened out of our wits at life itself. The proliferation of broadcast channels from only three companies but a few years ago—CBS, ABC, and NBC—to hundreds today has brought the reporting of tragedy into the sanctity of our homes 24-7. Because they are profit-driven corporations, each network makes every attempt to gain the competitive edge. This is accomplished primarily through well-calculated sensationalism aimed at promoting fear, gore, sex, drugs, explosions, scams, corruption, impending storms, crashes, shootings—a truth that anyone who watches the news on a regular basis can affirm. Every conceivable strategy is utilized to whip viewers into near panic regarding what has happened, is happening, or might happen to threaten their basic securities. The anxiety this causes the average person is immeasurable, so much so that it tends to lull us into a state of numbed complacency about matters of real concern.

To further compound matters, add in the brilliance of today's marketing gurus with their tools and abilities to exploit basic human instincts and needs with Madison Avenue strategies. The airwaves are literally bombarded with every gizmo and gadget, every food and beverage, every pharmaceutical and cosmetic, every insurance package and health plan that promise to bring us happiness. Through these advertisements the message is conveyed—overtly and subliminally—hundreds upon thousands of times that we are only one purchase away from nailing down the security that we are repeatedly led to believe is in serious jeopardy.

In short, we live in a cultural schizophrenia of sorts. We are caught in a perpetual state of tension and confusion between the media reminding us of the constant danger we live in, and the advertising industry pushing products at us, one right after the other, as the secret to finding the happiness we seek. In response, we have become a throwaway consumer society that is fast spreading this same value throughout the world. One wonders if our interest in pushing capitalism onto other countries is, as much as anything, a way to convince ourselves that consumer-mania is the answer to finding happiness. Deep down we all know that consuming more doesn't bring us lasting joy. The truth is that the more we get the more we want, because the more we get the more the cravings of our souls go unanswered.

In this state of material richness yet Spiritual emptiness, people are hurting, asking tough questions, and seeking answers.

–   Why don't I feel more joy in my life?

–   How do I control the anger or cope with the depression I feel due to all the things that go wrong in my life from day to day?

- What—and whom—can I trust anymore when there are so many conflicting opinions about the correct choices to make and the proper courses of action to follow?

- Is there any hope for our future, or the future of our children?

- How do I find peace of mind in desperate situations, such as loss of a job, the death of a loved one, or a life-threatening illness?

- How can I find happiness again?

- What is the meaning and purpose of life, where do I fit in, and what happens to us after we die?

Seek as they might, millions of people are not finding the answers that would fulfill them. Unimaginable advances in technology are leading to the globalization of everything. The result is a breaking down of old paradigms that once kept things mostly glued together. In the fast-changing world we live in today, many time-honored answers are becoming unglued, which leaves us in a chronic state of tension and insecurity. Something is clearly missing, and we must seek new answers that befit the times.

The answers are there. But if we are to find them, we must look in the right places. Predominantly we have sought happiness and hope externally—in things, in relationships, in food and drink, in money and possessions. As a species we have turned over many stones trying to find the elixir of life, a peace that passes understanding, the secret that would fill our souls.

But finding the answers *outside* ourselves is precisely the opposite of what every major religion and the great Spiritual Masters taught. Jesus said that the kingdom of God— and the peace, love, and joy that are part of that kingdom—are *within*. Buddha taught that all beings are imbued with a spark of *inner* divine light. The

Jewish mystics use similar words when they speak of the *inner* spark or the spark of God. The Koran talks about our Spiritual search which inevitably becomes a search for divine or sacred light. By cultivating our *inner* core, we search for this light in ourselves. For Hindus true reality lies *within*. The ultimate level of the transcendental state is pure awareness, in which we find Spiritual enlightenment. And in Taoism, to find God one must follow an individual path that comes from *within*.

* * *

A note is due here about the difference between religion and Spirituality. "Religion" is an organized system of beliefs, rites, and celebrations. It is based on faith in an absolute set of truths centered around a powerful supernatural being that is to be worshipped and obeyed. "Spirituality," on the other hand, is the quality or state of being "Spiritual," where Spiritual means of or related to the "Spirit." What, then, is "Spirit?" It is the vital principle or animating force believed to be within all living beings. Spirit is that in which we live and move and have our being.

When we go inside ourselves to discover the nature of Spirit, we are in effect launching an expedition in search of our source through self-awareness. We are looking within to explore what causes our anguish and suffering in order to free ourselves from it. Like Jules Verne's *Journey to the Center of the Earth*, Spirituality is about a journey to the center of our being. The original intent of all world religions and the Spiritual masters who founded them was to help people take this journey. In some religions today that intention no doubt still exists; in others it may not. That would be up to you to decide.

The fact is that we live in a time when rising numbers of people are more willing to call themselves "Spiritual" rather than "religious." In the words of contemporary Spiritual teacher Eckhart Tolle:[1]

...a growing number of followers of traditional religions are able to let go of identification with form, dogma, and rigid belief systems and discover the original depth that is hidden within their own [S]piritual tradition at the same time that they discover the depths within themselves. They realize that how "[S]piritual" you are has nothing to do with what you believe but everything to do with your state of consciousness. This, in turn, determines how you act in the world and interact with others.

This movement toward a new Spirituality may reflect our instinct to revere and respect that from which we came, which is Spirit. This is the reason why the word Spirit is capitalized throughout as a way to acknowledge its inherent sacredness. This holds true for its many derivatives as well: Spiritual, Spirituality, Spirit Consciousness, Spiritual Awareness, and Spiritual Consciousness, which will be used interchangeably throughout the book. Also, "Spirituality" is not intended to represent the beliefs or traditions of any particular religion, knowing full well that the essence of Spiritual truth is encased—however obscurely—in each of them.

For our purposes, *Beyond the Ego* is about Spirituality in that its focus is on the Spirit, which lies within. The entry point into that world is one's "self," that is, one's sense of "I"-ness, who "I" am. The word "I" is derived from the Latin word *ego*, so a journey into "I" is a journey into ego. When you go there you will find that most, if not all of our dissatisfaction and suffering can be traced directly or indirectly to ego. Once you fully understand how and why this is true and especially how and why it is true for you, then and only then are you ready to go beyond the ego into the world of Spirit where the peace and happiness you seek can truly be found.

What is this elusive something—the Spirit—that lies beyond the ego? How does one find it, and even more, how does one go about looking for it? Is it just for the mystics and the monks, or is it something the average person can do in the midst of frenetic schedules that impact so many of our lives? Will it help us deal with the fear and insecurity that confronts us in one way or another every single day? Does it have the potential to bring sanity back into our lives and restore happiness and hope for oneself as well as for humanity?

This book is written to help you answer each of these questions. It is, in effect, a road map to help you discover the truths embodied in the Spiritual traditions of nearly every world religion, but without the dogma and rituals that tend to mask them. These same truths will guide you to joy, happiness, peace of mind, and your divine source within—the light that shows the way. They are the hidden secrets that lay within you the reader, and within all of humankind. They lie dormant and are waiting to be awakened. For in their awakening we discover the solution to our personal, communal, and global troubles. We find the truth—the "light"—we all seek, the salvation from our errors, the liberation from the bonds of sorrow and suffering, and the freedom to be peaceful and happy souls.

Our search must take us into a place we don't normally go, but this is the only place where the answers can be found. That place is "within," and in order to go there we must first journey into the realm of the ego, and then beyond.

* * *

Lastly, a few comments on how you might consider reading this book. Most authors, no doubt, would prefer that you read the chapters sequentially, since that's the way the ideas unfolded in their minds to help you progress conceptually from beginning to end. But not everyone reads this way. Some people like to thumb through the chapters and read only the parts that look the most interesting or relevant. Some go to the end and read the summary or conclusion, and from there decide what they would like to learn more about. Still others look at the table of contents and then read the chapters that seem most likely to speak to them. With all due respect for the many different styles of reading, here are some things to keep in mind as you proceed.

Beyond the Ego is written in seven parts. When read sequentially, these parts build from one to the next to make the whole.

For readers who like to go straight to the nugget, it is recommended that you first finish Part I (*Introduction and Overview*). From there, Part III (*Experience Is the Teacher of All Things*), Part IV (*Ego Consciousness Is the Source of Dissatisfaction, Suffering, and Misery*), and Part V (*Spiritual Consciousness Is the Wellspring of Happiness, Joy, and Peace of Mind*) would be best read in that order.

Part II (*We Are All One*), and Part VI (*Spirit Has a Language of Its Own*) could conceivably be read as supplementary material in any order you'd like, if you are not inclined to read the chapters in the order presented. Part VII (*Conclusion*) is a summarization that recaps the main premises of the book.

Chapter Two

WHO WE ARE

Most people ask themselves at some point in their lives, "Who am I?" "Why am I here?" and "Where am I going?" The answer to each of these questions is the end goal of most philosophies and all religions. The answers, of course, vary greatly.

One attempt to address these questions is to ask, "Are we Spiritual beings having a physical experience or physical beings having a Spiritual experience?" My answer is neither. *We are Spiritual beings having an ego experience.* But what does this mean?

* * *

All that exists is derived from a single source of divine energy. Traditional religions believe this source of energy is the Supreme Being they worship. Examples include Jehovah in Christianity, Brahman in Hinduism, and Allah in Islam. In nontraditional religions, and in the secular world in general, this energy is often referred to as the Universe, the Source, the Force, or Reality. But there is only one world. So, in fact, these various names all describe the same thing.

For our purposes, this single source of energy is called Spirit, which is the same as Pure Consciousness. Spirit is the energy that runs the world. The original meaning of Spirit is "breath." Spirit is what brings us fully to life at birth when we take our first breath. It is what leaves our physical bodies when we breathe our last. Spirit is intangible and defies description. It cannot be comprehended logically or conceptually. Spirit can only be known by experiencing it at the feeling level. Anything that could possibly be said about it is like a road sign that helps point the way.

* * *

All things are born of the Spirit, which means they are born in a state of Pure Consciousness. Everything that exists is Spirit in its many manifestations: people, plants, animals and inanimate objects as well. Quantum physics has clearly demonstrated that even material things, long thought to be lifeless, are actually subatomic particles vibrating at an incredibly rapid rate of speed, which is characteristic of all forms of life.

All things nonhuman live *in* the Spirit, which is the same as saying they are conscious. But they are not aware of that fact. Human beings live *in* the Spirit as well, and hence are also conscious. There is one remarkable difference, however. We alone have the capacity for self-reflection—the faculty that allows us to be aware of our own consciousness; i.e., we can be conscious of our"selves."

Based on our early experiences in life, we have been conditioned to feel—and therefore, to believe—that my "self " is a separate, isolated being struggling for survival in an alien world. This is the consciousness level that one normally has of one's "self," which is called "ego." But it is a limiting consciousness because it isn't ultimately who we are. We are not separate and isolated beings in the world. We are all one, born of the Spirit and joined together by different manifestations of Pure Consciousness.

Unknowingly, we have erred as a species in defining who we are in relation to the world. We have missed the mark or missed the point of our existence. This mistaken identity has become the infrastructure for our beliefs, our language, and our ways of thinking, relating, and being. Consequently, and over time, an ever-widening gap has developed between who we think we are—ego—and who we really are—Spirit. The result is a growing state of tension for humankind that makes life stressful, disconcerting, and oftentimes miserable.

Said differently, we are born of the Spirit in Pure Consciousness. Early experiences in life lead us to believe that our ability to self-reflect is limited to one level of awareness—ego consciousness. As a result of that belief, we fall from Pure Consciousness into a state of ego consciousness, which is a repository for discontentment, anguish, and suffering.

Humanity is not doomed to stay there, however. There is a purer, more peaceful, and more joyful level of consciousness that we are all capable of reaching, and that is to enter the realm of Spiritual Consciousness. *Spiritual Consciousness is a return to our source—an experience of holy oneness—which is characterized by freedom, peace, and love in this life and beyond.*

* * *

Spirit *is*. It is eternal and everlasting. We humans are a unique expression of Spirit with the capacity to be conscious of "self" not only at the ego level, but at the Spirit level as well. Once we achieve Spirit Consciousness, we see with great clarity that ego consciousness is hell. Knowing this intellectually is one thing; experiencing Spirit in all its fullness is quite another. Once we enter the world of Spirit, which is the same as becoming more Spiritual, a major, but subtle shift occurs in our state of being. It is an internal change that cannot help but reflect itself on the outside as well. It is the joy and peace that we begin to experience in life at all times, wherever we are and regardless of what we're doing.

This, then, is our destiny as human beings: to become conscious that we are more than ego, that we are not stuck in pain, and that we are meant to live, love, and be happy. This consciousness is the meeting ground where Spirit and Pure Consciousness merge into one. They were never separate, really, except as ego made it so.

The vast majority of humanity has never gone beyond their ego "selves"—never experienced the freedom, exhilaration, and heartfelt joy of living. The reasons are twofold. First, until fairly recently, people were generally not aware of the relationship between Spirit and ego. Not knowing, we got stuck in the limited awareness of ego consciousness and have proceeded to live our lives in the misery and heartache that go with it. Second, we are best positioned to go beyond ego when our personal suffering reaches its limit, or when we become sufficiently sensitized to the very real risk of annihilation as a species, or both. For growing numbers of people, that time has come.

* * *

Who are we then? Again, *we are Spiritual beings having an ego experience.* That is, we are ego selves until we get beyond the ego, at which point we rediscover our Spiritual selves. This is who we really are—Pure Consciousness. This is the realm where we find happiness, peace, and joy.

You deserve these things; they are your birthrights. They will be yours once you learn how to get beyond the constraints of ego. For some individuals the first steps of this transition will happen rather quickly. For others it might take a little longer. Know, however, that your journey beyond the ego and into Spirit is one where each step along the way will bring you undeniable internal rewards—ones that will be sufficient for most people to compel them to continue the journey until it is completed.

The best news is that getting started is actually quite simple. But first, we need to lay the conceptual foundation that prepares you to begin your journey, which is next.

Part II

We Are All One

Chapter Three

THE BIG BANG

Several years ago I was waiting in an airport to catch a flight. Suddenly and for no apparent reason I was struck by a compelling thought that "it's all about consciousness." It was the kind of experience—perhaps you've had one like it—where you just shake your head as if to ask, "What was that?" I didn't know at the time, and though that same thought would come back to me again and again like a dream that you can't quite forget, it would be some time before I would come to know exactly what it meant.

That time came when I began to learn about discoveries being made in the field of quantum physics. Within that discipline, it is now an accepted fact—and admittedly this is a very elementary summary of a hugely complex subject—that everything in the universe is but a collection of atomic and subatomic particles comprised of nuclei, electrons, and protons that create vibrational energies. At some moment in time, something approximately the size of a pea exploded—the Big Bang—and created the zillions of differences that comprise the universe as we now know it. In other words, we all came from the same stuff contained in that pea-sized something. The only real difference between this and that, an oak tree and a Dalmatian, a lamppost and a rose, is the frequency at which different energies vibrate.

What was that "something" from which everything stems? Amit Goswami,[1] a theoretical quantum physicist, offers this answer:

> The current worldview has it that *everything is made of matter*, and everything can be reduced to the elementary particles of matter, the basic constituents—building blocks—of matter...elementary particles make atoms, atoms make molecules, molecules make cells, and cells make brain. But all the way, the ultimate cause is always the interactions between the elementary particles. This is the belief—all cause moves from the elementary particles. This is what we call "upward causation."
>
> ...Now, the opposite view is that *everything starts with consciousness*. That is, *consciousness is the ground of all being*. In this view, consciousness imposes "downward causation."

* * *

This is the first and most basic lesson to learn about Spirituality because it is the epicenter of nearly every Spiritual tradition: ***Everything is made of the same conscious "stuff"; this is one universe; all of life is one; and where there are differences, there is ultimately no separation between the parts and pieces.***

* * *

Broadly speaking, there are four categories of consciousness, with the fourth being subdivided into two different types:

- Material Consciousness
- Plant Consciousness
- Animal Consciousness
- Human Consciousness

- ○ Ego Consciousness
- ○ Spiritual Consciousness

This book is primarily about ego consciousness and Spiritual Consciousness. Getting beyond the first is your entrance into the second, where happiness abounds. Before we go there, a brief discussion about the nonhuman dimensions of consciousness will help deepen our understanding of the essential unity of all things. This unity, in the end, is the essence of Spirituality.

* * *

But first a word about "categorizing," which is as risky a venture as it is convenient. The mind loves to categorize things, since it helps to make sense of the big picture by breaking it into smaller pieces. The risk is that such an exercise can easily imply "separation" between the parts. In an everything-is-made-of-the-same-stuff model of the universe, there is no such thing as separation. Things are different, one from the other, but they are not separate.

It is further characteristic of the mind to arrange categories into hierarchies wherever possible—from top to bottom, superior to inferior, most to least, best to worst, or vice versa. Yet we must be extremely cautious about this distinctly human quality to judge one thing as better or worse than another. Many argue that the ability to do so proves the superiority of us humans over all else on the earth. This may be so, but it could be equally argued that it proves nothing more than our tendency toward egocentricity.

Therefore, in the discussion that follows, there is expressly no intent to presume or imply that any one state of consciousness is superior or inferior to the others. In the words of Ken Wilber,[2] who is one of the most comprehensive philosophical and spiritual thinkers of our time, "There is nothing…but Spirit in all directions, and not a grain of sand, not a speck of dust, is more or less Spirit than any other." All consciousness is cut from the same cloth, so to speak, yet the form and shape each takes is different.

While it may seem like Spiritual Consciousness has been previously positioned to be superior to ego consciousness, this is not the intent. The fact is that Spiritual Consciousness is a happier and more peaceful place than ego consciousness, but this is not to say that one *should* go there. It is a choice everyone must make for him or herself. When we become aware that there is a choice, most people will choose happiness over suffering, but some may not be ready to make that choice. There is no necessity to do so, and there is no judgment made about the choice one ultimately makes. What else could it mean to have free will?

Also you will notice that no definition of consciousness has as yet been offered. This is intentional because we know so little about it. For many readers, a definition of sorts may well emerge as your awareness of the different states of consciousness unfolds.

Chapter Four

MATERIAL CONSCIOUSNESS

We are not accustomed to thinking of material things as being conscious, so to some readers this may seem at first like a perfectly odd idea. It is not a new one, however. It has actually been around throughout the history of philosophy, and, in fact, has played a large influence in it. Examples include the work of Alfred North Whitehead, Albert Einstein, and William James. The notion of material consciousness is unfamiliar in part because the concept is rarely named.

There is a name for it, nonetheless. It is called "panpsychism," which is the notion that all parts of matter involve consciousness (Spirit), or more holistically, the view that the whole universe is an organism that possesses Pure Consciousness at every level. Dr. Ken Van Cleve,[1] an expert on the subject of panpsychism, writes that:

> Panpsychism declares that the entire universe from the most distant galaxy all the way down to the smallest particle or wave is entirely sentient or conscious. They are all connected parts of the whole. Panpsychists believe that *all matter* in the universe has some degree of consciousness.

In other words, the substance of the universe is composed entirely of...Consciousness.

This [consciousness] is in you and me, the most distant star, the smallest subatomic particle or wave, and we are all connected. Not only are we connected but also every particle within each entity is aware of all the other particles. We are all part of a grand communication scheme that is the "Glue" that holds the universe together.

Jim Holt,[2] a contributing writer to *The Times Magazine*, wrote the following in his article, "Mind of a Rock":

Perhaps [consciousness] is not limited to the brains of some animals. Perhaps it is ubiquitous, present in every bit of matter, all the way up to the galaxies, all the way down to electrons and neutrinos, not excluding medium-size things like a glass of water or a potted plant....

Take that rock over there. It doesn't seem to be doing much of anything, a least to our gross perception. But at the micro level it consists of an unimaginable number of atoms connected by springy chemical bonds, all jiggling around at a rate that even our fastest supercomputer might envy. And they are not jiggling at random. The rock's innards "see" the entire universe by means of the gravitational and electromagnetic signals it is continuously receiving. Such a system can be viewed as an all-purpose information processor, one whose inner dynamics mirror any sequence of mental states that our brains might run through. And where there is information....there is consciousness...

But the rock doesn't exert itself as a result of all this "thinking." Why should it? Its existence, unlike ours, doesn't depend on the struggle to survive and self-replicate. It is indifferent to the prospect of being pulverized. If you are poetically inclined, you might think of the rock as a purely contemplative being.

Christian de Quincey, Ph.D.,[3] a philosopher and author who teaches consciousness, spirituality, and cosmology at universities and colleges in the United States and internationally, writes the following:

> ...science may be seriously mistaken when it asserts that consciousness is a product of complex brains and that the rest of vital nature is a product of mindless, purposeless, unfeeling evolution. We may not be so special.

> ...the path to the sacred may not be through priests or churches. In my experience, the sacred is all around us in nature. You can encounter the sacred by watching a sunset, playing with animals, walking through a forest or on a beach, swimming in the ocean, climbing a mountain, planting flowers or vegetables, filling your lungs with fresh air, smelling the mulch of rich nourishing soil, dancing through crackling autumn leaves, comforting an injured pet, embracing a loved one, or holding the hand of a dying parent. The most direct way to God, I believe, is through touching and feeling the Earth and its inhabitants and being open to the expression of Spirit in the most ordinary, as well as the most awesome, events of daily life. The way to meaning is reconnection with the world of nature through exuberant participation or through the stillness of meditation, just being present and listening. When you do so, you hear, you feel, and you learn: you are not alone; you are not uniquely special.

For the most part, neither mainstream science nor conventional religion recognizes that humans are not essentially different from the rest of nature. Both regard matter and the world of nature as "dumb." Both assert that human beings are somehow special and stand apart from nature because, they say, only human beings—or at least creatures with brains and nervous systems—have consciousness or souls. On the contrary, I say, consciousness goes all the way down.

Contrary to what's taught in science today, consciousness is not produced by brains. In fact, you don't even need a brain to have a mind. All animals, all plants, even bacteria have something we would call "mind." I'm saying that all bodies of any kind have consciousness "all the way down" to atoms and beyond to quarks, or quanta, or whatever lies at the root of physical reality. In this view, all of nature—all matter—tingles with the spark of [S]pirit.

This uncommon view, called "panpsychism," presents a radical and controversial account of the relationship between bodies and minds, between matter and souls.... The new view I'm proposing is that matter feels, matter is sentient, matter has experience, and matter is adventurous. It probes and directs its way through the long, winding path of evolution. From its first appearance after the Big Bang—from the first atom, molecule, and cell—to the magnificence and glory of the human brain, the great unfolding of evolution is literally the story the universe is telling to itself. The cosmos is enacting the greatest epic drama imaginable. Truly, it is the greatest story ever told. And humankind is just one of the storytellers. In the evolution of the cosmos, matter itself is the prime storyteller.

We need to develop a deep respect for nature because it is the source of everything we are. Like each of us, all of nature has a mind of its own. This is because matter is not at all what science thinks it to be. Matter is not dead stuff.

Matter feels. The very stuff of our bodies, the very stuff of the Earth, tingles with its own sentience. It is time for us to rediscover the soul of matter, to honor and respect the flesh of the Earth, to pay attention to the meaning, purpose, and value embedded in the world beneath our feet and above our heads. Maybe then we will save ourselves from the otherwise inevitable ecological and civilizational collapse that faces us in our lifetime.

Chapter Five

PLANT CONSCIOUSNESS

As with material consciousness, plant consciousness may be on a level so different from our own that our prejudice renders us unable to recognize it as such. That it exists, however, is a tenet held by many people both inside and outside of the scientific community. For fear of being seen as "kooks," many individuals the world over have remained relatively silent about being able to communicate with plants. Even so, there are documented reports from many plant lovers that their plants respond to positive attention, such as when they talk gently to them or play soft music.

Clearly the growth patterns of plants demonstrate that they respond to physical stimuli. Photosynthesizing plants grow toward light and climbing plants grow in ways that are compatible with their supporting structure. But does this by itself make them conscious? In an article entitled "Plants as Sensitive Agents," Charles Allon,[1] former director of Borderland Sciences, writes the following:

> Do plants engage in dynamic conscious dialogue with the ground and other beings? Empirical discoveries made throughout the century by notables such as Bose, Hieronymus, De LaWarr, Backster, Lawrence, and others give

adequate proof of this dialogue….The remarkable sensitivity of plants to external conscious and auric influences is providing us all with a revolutionary new means of experimentation….We may hypothesize that plants collectively respond to a specified range which includes sensual, emotive, and semi-conscious variations.

In summarizing her understanding of certain points made by Tompkins and Bird in their book *The Secret Life of Plants,* Susan Barber,[2] a writer for the online magazine *Spirit of Ma'at,* comments that:

…Christopher Bird and Peter Tompkins revealed literally centuries worth of hard facts supporting that plants—in fact, everything in creation—are conscious, intelligent, and aware of human beings and each other…

…If asked the difference between plants and animals, many of us would respond that animals are free to move about, whereas plants are not. This is the first misconception exploded by Tompkins and Bird. The truth, they explain, is that…trees and other plants simply live in a different phase of time than we do. To prove to ourselves that plants move, all we need to do is emulate the work of the Viennese biologist Raoul Francé and take time-lapse photographs. Then, as he did, we will see plants creeping or growing—intelligently and perceptively, but very, very slowly—toward or away from things that support or threaten them.

According to Tompkins and Bird, the whole scientific uproar about plant communication began in 1966 when Cleve Baxter—then America's foremost lie-detector examiner—decided on impulse to attach his polygraph electrodes to the now-famous dracaena (plant) in his office, then water the plant and see if the leaves responded.

Finding that the plant indeed reacted to this event, he decided to see what would happen if he threatened it, and formed in his mind the idea of lighting a match to the leaf where the electrodes were attached.

And that was when something happened that forever changed Baxter's life and ours. For the plant didn't wait for him to light the match. *It reacted to his thoughts!* Through further research, Baxter found that it was his intent, and not merely the thought itself, that brought about this reaction.

He also discovered that plants were aware of each other, mourned the death of anything (even the bacteria killed when boiling water is poured down the drain), strongly disliked people who killed plants carelessly or even during scientific research, and fondly remembered and extended their energy out to people who had grown and tended them, even when their "friends" were far away in both time and space.

...[and] Yes, it's true. Plants don't like rock music. When it's played to them, they bend sharply away from the source. Over a long time, it can kill them. But plants do like classical music and, perhaps surprisingly, jazz. When that type of music is played to a field of crops, more and heavier grain is produced than in control fields that receive no serenades.

In addition to respecting the expertise of coauthors Tompkins and Bird, it is key to the understanding of the probable consciousness of plants to be reminded that Cleve Baxter was not some crackpot with eccentric ideas about plants. In 1966, he was America's leader in lie detection who taught classes to various police departments and security organizations on how to use the polygraph device. His instrument was a galvanometer (lie detector), and movement of the inked needle on a roll of paper indicated that the person being examined was experiencing stress.

When applied to humans, the presence of stress indicated the likelihood that the person being examined was lying. But when Baxter used a galvanometer to measure the minute electrical signals from plants, he found by means of the same movement of the needle that he could determine their responses to various stimuli and situations.

Over the next thirty years Baxter conducted numerous experiments to demonstrate that plants and humans share similar response patterns. Plants have positive and negative emotional responses to their physical and "mental" environments just like we do. In fact, Baxter discovered from his experiments that plants are even more capable than most humans in at least one respect: plants are capable of telepathy or "reading the minds" of the other beings in their environment. They form bonds with certain individuals and are capable of knowing their intentions.

Crazy ideas? Many say yes, which is understandable because it defies conventional wisdom, at least here in the West. And for some, the thought that plants have consciousness threatens the importance of humanity's place in the universe.

But there are experts on the subject of plant consciousness, whose findings are, for them, proof positive that plants are sensitive and responsive to external stimuli—including sound and human intention. Gradually rising numbers of people in the Western world are coming to the awareness that we are, in fact, all one, and for many of them the notion that plants exhibit a state of consciousness is self-evident: they are part of the thread of consciousness—the Spirit—running through all of life.

Chapter Six

ANIMAL CONSCIOUSNESS

Much debate occurs between psychologists, philosophers, behavioral scientists, and animal activists over the question, "Do nonhuman animals (hereafter, 'animals') have consciousness?" Many pet owners would think this to be a silly question and would answer with a resounding "of course!" One can hardly be licked on the nose by a puppy, or sit while one's cat purrs on his or her lap, or experience the incredible bond between horse and rider while galloping through the fields, without wondering why such a simple question requires so much debate.

The reason is that animals have more characteristics in common with humans than rocks or plants do. So the question takes on added importance as we attempt to better understand our own place in the bigger scheme of things.

Probably the most debated question about animal consciousness is not whether animals are conscious, but "are they conscious in the same way that humans are?" Interestingly, framing the question in this way assumes that animals *are* conscious, which is precisely the point.

Certainly, they are not conscious in exactly the same ways humans are, just as plants are not conscious in the same way as rocks. To those who wrestle with this question, the answer depends on how one defines "consciousness." Part of the difficulty in settling the debate is the shear number of definitions of the word. But remember, consciousness is purposely not defined in this discussion. To define anything is to limit and confine, and we want to do neither. We want simply to stay open to what consciousness is and let our understanding of it unfold as we work our way through its various levels of expression.

* * *

Since this is not a scientific textbook on biology, liberty is taken for "animal" to mean every living nonhuman creature from the simplest to the most complex, from the amoeba to the primate. Clearly there is a gigantic gap between the simple responses of the amoeba and the thought processes and sentience of more complex species. Still, just to make a point, science writer Colin Barras, Ph.D.,[1] writes that: "Amoebas are smarter than they look…In recent years, the humble amoeba has surprised researchers with its ability to behave in an 'intelligent' way…which suggests the cells have a rudimentary memory."

This is especially curious when you couple it with a comment cell biologist Bruce Lipton[2] makes in his book *The Biology of Belief.* "You may consider yourself an individual, but as a cell biologist, I can tell you that you are in truth a cooperative community of approximately fifty trillion single-celled citizens. Almost all the cells that make up your body are amoeba-like, individual organisms that have evolved a cooperative strategy for their mutual support. Reduced to basic terms, human beings are simply the consequence of 'collective amoebic consciousness'."

As for the more complex of the animals, few people would disagree that they experience a wide range of feelings, from pain and depression to excitement and joy. They interact, they learn, and to some degree they think. These four characteristics—thinking, feeling, interacting, and learning—are surely evidence that higher-order animals have consciousness.

Russell Dewey, Ph.D., [3] a psychology professor, speaks to this issue as it relates specifically to animals' feelings:

It is probably fair to assume that non-human animals have a sort of nonlinguistic consciousness. This seems obvious to many pet owners and people well acquainted with species like horses that interact intelligently with humans.

Most mammals have limbic systems that rival the size of human limbic systems, in proportion to their brains, and the limbic system is the seat of emotion. With experience, it is easy to get to know and understand the emotions of almost any mammalian species. Sociable birds such as parrots and penguins also seem remarkably transparent in their feelings and motives to people who know them well.

And to the same point, from an unknown author:[4]

Humans share the planet with as many as 4,700 species of mammals, 9,700 species of birds, 4,800 species of amphibians, over 23,000 species of fish and around 6,000 species of reptiles (as far as we know up to now), not to mention the countless species of invertebrate animals. We interact with and use animals in a multitude of ways in our daily lives….[and] they are very complex and important to our understanding of the place of humans in the natural world.

A huge increase in scientific research on animal sentience is beginning to answer some of the questions about animal sentience and animal consciousness…The most basic way of experiencing the world is through feeling or sensation. "Sentience" is defined as the ability to have perceptions and sensations. A "sentient animal" is an animal that is aware of his/her surroundings and of what happens to him/her and is capable of feeling pain and pleasure, at the least. The current scientific consensus is that all vertebrate animals, at least, are capable of feeling pain and experiencing distress….

But many of the animals we interact with turn out to have more complex mental and emotional lives than people have understood in the past, and new scientific research is constantly revealing new evidence of animals' cognitive abilities and their emotions.

Sentient animals have preferences and intentions….They can maintain complex social relationships in their groups. Some animals can understand what another animal is going to do, and attempt to deceive that animal in order to gain an advantage. Some animals can enjoy learning a new skill. Some animals react to other animals in ways resembling human empathy. On the negative side, animals can experience the unpleasant emotions of pain, fear, frustration, and probably boredom as well. They can be reduced to a state resembling human depression by chronic stress or confinement in a cage.

All these abilities listed above have been documented in scientific research. Of course these abilities vary between different species.… Several of the abilities that have in the past been thought to be uniquely human, for example, the use of tools, the ability to plan ahead, the ability to empathize with another or to deceive another, the transmission of skills in ways that can be classified as "culture" behavior that can be classified as "morality"—are now known to exist to some extent among nonhuman animals too. From the point of view of evolutionary biology, it makes sense that humans should share many *of our emotional and cognitive abilities with some of the other animal species.*

The point is that our collective experience with a wide variety of animals, plain old common sense, and a number of scientific advances in animal studies all point to the obvious— *animals are indeed conscious beings.* As with all things, they are born of the Spirit in a state of Pure Consciousness. They experience and express their consciousness all in their own way, just as do material objects and plants. In many ways animals are conscious like humans, especially in terms of their ability to feel a wide range of emotions.

* * *

There remains one unique difference between nonhuman animals and us humans, however, and that is our ability to abstract ourselves in thought; that is, we can think about ourselves—our thoughts, feelings, and experiences. More specifically, abstraction is the thought process wherein ideas are distanced from objects. You and I can see a ball, then close our eyes and think about the ball that we just saw. Presumably an animal cannot do this. Even if this is false, you and I can think about a time when a ball might have been thrown to us, but a dog most likely cannot. A dog can lay by the door waiting for its owner to arrive home, which gives the appearance of the dog thinking about its owner, or perhaps even wondering where the owner is en route. But this is more likely a hunger pain or a limbic response to missing its master rather than remembering what that person was wearing when he or she left the house or what will be served for dinner.

And even in the unlikely event that some animals can think about an object distanced from them, what seems altogether obvious is that they cannot think about their own thoughts and emotions. If they could, a dog that is afraid of a thunderstorm, for example, would act similarly afraid if it could recall the thunderstorm that happened last week, which by all appearances isn't the case. In other words, the dog's behavior is a response to the moment—a primary response—not a secondary response from anticipating that the same event may reoccur.

The reason for making a point of our capability to abstract ourselves in thought is that abstraction is, simultaneously, a gift and a burden. The gift is obvious: we can think, remember, predict, create, plan, reflect, anticipate—all the cognitive functions that we perform every day. The burden is, abstraction is the mother of ego, and ego is the source of our dissatisfaction and suffering.

Yet just as abstraction creates ego, so can abstraction get us beyond it. For now, if you can reach some level of comfort that we are all made of the same conscious "stuff," and therefore that we are all one—different, but not separate, you are then ready to embark on your journey beyond the ego into the world of happiness and peace of mind.

Part III

Experience Is the Teacher of All Things

–Julius Caesar

Chapter Seven

HOW WE LEARN

We are about to begin our journey into and beyond the ego. In preparation, the first lesson to learn about ego is that it is elusive, subtle, and slippery. It is a moving target that is difficult to freeze-frame long enough to take its picture. Still, it is possible to capture the nature and function of ego if we first are fully grounded in the process of how we learn.

Learning is the modification of behavior by experience. More specifically, learning is the process where a living being experiences certain relationships between thoughts, feelings, and events and is able to recognize an association between them. Subsequently, there is a change in the subject's behavior as a result of that experience.

* * *

A candle burns on an end table in the family room while the parents watch TV. It catches the attention of their eighteen-month-old child, who toddles over and reaches out to touch the flame. It burns his little hand, and he cries out in pain. The parents rush to soothe the child, treat the burn, and tell him, "You mustn't put your hand in the fire; it is hot and will burn you!" From that point forth, the child avoids coming in direct contact with fire. He has learned.

Encased in this scenario lies the primal blueprint for how experience is the teacher of all things. All feelings, thoughts, and behaviors result from the experiences we have and the associations we make as a result of those experiences. The child's experience (touching the flame) led to feelings (pain, hurt, fear), which led to thoughts (don't touch fire), which led to new behavior (avoidance of contact with fire). Experiences cause feelings; feelings cause thoughts; thoughts cause changes in behavior.

Experiences → Feelings → Thoughts → Behaviors

* * *

This formula is not the be-all and end-all in theories about how we learn. As our brains develop and mature, many more factors come into play: styles of learning, levels of intelligence, the role of didactics and rote memorization, classical and operant conditioning, social influences, and much more.

But this is not a textbook on complex learning theories. It is a Spiritual guide to help us get beyond the ego in order to find a more peaceful and meaningful existence. Accomplishing this requires an awareness of where all learning starts, especially as it relates to what we learn in the earliest years of our lives. Unless something is done to reverse the impact of these early experiences—which is the goal of this book—they profoundly shape how we feel, think, and behave ever after. We will discover in part IV how ego develops from our experiences early on, and how it subsequently shapes our lives in ways that can cause us much pain and suffering.

* * *

Another example: The mother of a young girl was always too busy sewing to spend time with her daughter. Feeling this void, the girl approached her mother one day and announced that she also would like to take up sewing. Her mother was warmed by the idea. She gave her daughter a hug and told her how happy this made her feel. Subsequently, the mother patiently taught her daughter the art of sewing. The girl loved the connection this created with her mother, and hence learned rapidly all that her mother could teach her. In the ensuing months and years, she entered several sewing competitions and often won the top award for her fine work.

In this instance there are actually two tiers of primal learning.

Tier one: Experience (lack of attention from her mother) led to feelings (I'm not special), led to thoughts (I want to sew too), led to behavior (telling her wishes to her mother).

Tier two: Experience (mother's favorable response) led to feelings (I am special), led to thoughts (I like to sew), led to behavior (entering and winning sewing competitions).

Experiences → Feelings → Thoughts → Behaviors

* * *

You might wish to pause and see how this formula of learning has worked in your own life.

- Have you ever stepped on the scales and discovered that you'd gained twenty pounds (experience)? Were you shocked (feelings)? Did you decide you needed to lose weight (thought)? Did you change your diet or increase you exercise (behavior)?

- Perhaps you took a course in college where you particularly respected and admired a professor (experience). This may have endeared you to the subject matter being taught (feelings). You decided you wanted to become a student of that same subject (thoughts). You changed your major and earned your degree in the same field of study (behavior).

— Maybe you were an only child and always wanted a brother or sister to play with (experience). As a result you were lonely (feelings). You remember thinking that you didn't want a child of yours to endure the same experience (thought). So you married and raised several children (behavior).

— Were you made to clean the house by yourself for years when you were a child (experience)? Did you dislike having to do so (feelings)? Did you think that as an adult you would never allow yourself to be put in a position where you had to clean the house without help (thought)? Did you hire a housekeeper after you were grown, or perhaps reach an agreement with your spouse that he or she would help with the cleaning (behavior)?

You will find as you check the truth of this formula that, in fact, experience *is* the teacher of all things. The rule never fails. It is certainly true that the same experience for different people may lead to different feelings, and therefore to different thoughts, and hence to different behaviors. But the principle that experience will always lead to feelings, thoughts, and behaviors of one kind or another is unerring.

* * *

Keep this definition of how we learn in mind as we begin to unravel the mystery of the ego. It is foundational that you do so, which is why this concept has been repeated and emphasized so pointedly here. Utilizing it allows us to look ego straight in the eye and see why we suffer personally, where our hurt comes from, why the world is in such a confused and troubled state, and what we can do to find the peace and happiness that we all seek and deserve.

Part IV

Ego Consciousness
Is the Source of
Dissatisfaction,
Suffering, and Misery

Chapter Eight

THE ORIGIN OF EGO

In the dictionary, "ego" is Latin for "I" (and its derivatives me, my, mine, myself). In real life the definition of "ego" isn't nearly as neat and tidy. The word has been so liberally interpreted that a definition which meets with widespread agreement is difficult to lock into.

Beginning in the late eighteen hundreds, when ego was first proposed as part of a person's mental apparatus, the field of psychology has given ego a fair amount of respect. Freud defined it as the arbitrator between the id and the superego. Jung called ego the center of consciousness that is responsible for one's feeling of identity and continuity. Therapists might assess a client as having a weak ego, which usually describes a person who lacks the emotional strength to deal with the normal stressors in life. They would think of a strong ego as just the opposite.

In common-language usage, ego hasn't been given nearly this same respect. "His ego got in the way" is a common expression to mean "His feelings of self-importance interfered with what he was trying to accomplish." Some people are said to have "big" egos, meaning they are rather full of themselves. Others might be described as being on an "ego trip," which suggests they have said or done something to increase their own power and influence or to draw attention to their own importance. And still others are labeled "egocentric," meaning they think of themselves as being so important that everything revolves around them, as the planets revolve around the sun. Interestingly, these kinds of labels are more often assigned to men than to women, though perhaps unfairly since having an ego has nothing to do with gender.

This propensity to equate ego with an inflated sense of self-importance represents a very narrow definition of ego, and also adds to the tendency to vilify it. It is often referred to as a delusion, an illusion, a trickster, a state of dysfunction or madness, or a deceptive and false identification as if it were a demon living inside us, an enemy that must be tamed, conquered, crushed, or overcome.

The truth is that ego is not any of these things—not a delusion, not an illusion, not a dysfunction or a madness, not deceptive and false, not a trickster, and not something to be conquered, overthrown, or overcome. To think of it as such pits you against it, as if at war. But this is impossible, because to a large degree, you *are* it.

* * *

Ego is not a place or a thing. It is a state of consciousness. (Hereafter, "ego" and "ego consciousness" are used interchangeably.) Ego is not something that lives in us; it is a large part of who we are. It is where the masses of humanity, past and present, live. Ego consciousness is where people are "in their heads" when awake. It is what's usually meant by consciousness itself. It is what people mean when they say I, me, my, mine, and myself. For the vast majority of people, ego is how we experience our everyday existence. It is our normal thinking and feeling state. It is the usual sensation one has of "I-myself."

* * *

We are not born with an ego. It is learned. Experience being the teacher of all things, we learn ego consciousness based on a common shared experience that we all have shortly after birth. This shared *experience* causes *feelings* that lead to *thoughts* that generate *behaviors*. In other words, ego develops through the four stages of primal learning:

Experiences → *Feelings* → *Thoughts* → *Behaviors.*

The Shared Experience

Ego development is entirely an unconscious phenomenon. It begins soon after a child is named. For ease of discussion, let's say that a newborn child is named "Emily" (knowing, of course, that this name actually stands for all human beings). In the following days, weeks, months, and years *Emily's experience will be that having a separate name and a separate body makes her a separate being.* She is Emily, her parents are Mommy and Daddy, the cat is Princess, and the dog is Duke. Each has his or her own name and body. Therefore each must be separate from the other.

Experience Causes Feelings

Given Emily's experience as a separate being, she will gradually develop the sensation that "I-myself" am an isolated person who exists apart from the rest of the world. *This sensation of disconnectedness causes feelings of smallness, insignificance, unimportance, and irrelevance. These feelings are the DNA of ego consciousness. "I" am a separate center of feeling and action, living inside my body, interacting with an "external" world of people and things that are large, alien, and strange.*

Emily's feelings of disconnectedness, insignificance, and smallness cause her to attach to her name and to her body as a way to feel connected and to fortify her existence. These early attachments will begin a lifelong quest of attaching to things, people, ideas, and beliefs in search of the security that she senses was lost in her experience of separateness.

Feelings Lead to Thoughts (Beliefs, Opinions, Judgments)

The feeling of separateness does not end in having a name and a body and attaching to them. It is a sensation that is reinforced repeatedly as the normal way of being, since everyone is in the same boat, so to speak. It is the result of having been taught to think in the language of disconnectedness as handed down from one's culture. This language is repeated and reinforced so often and in so many ways that it becomes a way of thinking that permeates our lives and takes us over. It is the ego developing.

In other words, the development and reinforcement of ego consciousness is predominantly a social phenomenon. Others close to Emily will condition her to become who she is and isn't, and how she should and shouldn't feel, think, and behave. The message that she is, indeed, a separate being is conveyed through the attitudes, words, values, and actions of others. As a case in point, the word "you" as it is often used with children can, by itself, imply Emily's separateness. "You are a naughty little girl" or "You are an angel"; it doesn't matter. Both suggest that her sense of "I"—her ego—is separate from others.

As Emily grows in years, she will be influenced by a number of social institutions that promote her belief in ego separateness. Public and private schools, for example, will teach her to be independent and self-reliant. "Think for yourself!" "Don't copy your friends!" "Be your own person!" "Get a grip on yourself!" Additionally, if Emily is brought up in the Judeo-Christian tradition, she will be taught—or allowed to believe—that God is a personal deity living "outside" of the world. This same notion encourages Emily, although subtly, to think that—like God—she is a separate entity existing apart from the rest of the universe.

* * *

The belief in separateness—albeit unconscious—contradicts logic and all available evidence. We were not born as separate beings—different, yes; separate, no. One does not at birth "come into" the world as much as one "grows out of" it, as roses from a bush. Alan Watts,[1] a British philosopher, writer, and speaker, expresses this succinctly in *The Book*: "As the ocean 'waves,' the universe 'peoples.' Every individual is an expression of the whole realm of nature, a unique action of the total universe."

His point is that we are all inextricably connected, since all things—including us humans—come from the same Spirit, the same conscious "stuff." *But when we believe that we are separate from this "stuff," then we believe that we are different beings than we really are. And that means we must try to make ourselves into something that we're really not.*

Think of it like this. If a squirrel could think it's a fish, it would try to act like a fish, though obviously with much distress. If a bird could think it's a turtle, it would try to act like a turtle, again with much distress. Behavior is always consistent with the thoughts that drive it. It is the same with humankind. If we think we're separate beings, then we will try to act like separate beings, even though we're not. But as with the squirrel and the bird, so with us: the results in each case will be dissatisfaction, suffering, and misery because these thoughts lead to behaviors that are neither consistent with nor conducive to who we really are.

Thoughts Lead to Behaviors

To define ourselves as separate from and alien to an unfriendly world is to have little choice but to behave in ways aimed at getting one up on the universe and everything in it. In other words, to fully act as isolated and disconnected beings, we must prepare for a lifelong battle in the struggle called "one-upmanship"—a superiority contest that for the sake of survival pits us one against the other.

One-upmanship is not to be equated with self-importance, per se. Wayne Dyer, Ph.D.,[2] an internationally renowned author and speaker in the field of self-development, speaks to the issue of self-importance in his book, *The Power of Intention*:

> Basically, your feelings of self-importance are what make you feel special…It's essential that you have a strong self-concept and that you feel unique. The problem is when you misidentify who you truly are by identifying yourself as your body, your achievements, and your possessions. Then you identify people who have accomplished less as inferior, and your self-important superiority causes you to be constantly offended in one way or another. This misidentification is the source of most of your problems, as well as most of the problems of humankind…With the self [ego] as a focal point, you sustain the illusion that you are your body, which is a completely separate entity from all others. This sense of separateness leads you to compete rather than cooperate with everyone else.

The sense of separateness that leads you to compete rather than cooperate is the sum and substance of one-upmanship. It is a feeling of superiority that becomes a constant source of friction and conflict between people at all conceivable levels. Sooner or later, it yields unhappy and sometimes disastrous results. The issue is always about who's right, who's the most important, who has the most power and influence, who's the wealthiest, who is highest on the social ladder, and so on. Couples and families often argue bitterly over such matters. Colleagues maneuver against one another to gain the next promotion. Neighbors stop speaking to each other over the slightest infractions. Politicians start rumors about their opponents to set them up for failure. People suffer from chronic insomnia, ulcers, and heart attacks from working long hours just to get ahead. And then there is the fallout from those who lose the battles: anger, depression, illnesses, and suicides.

These consequences and many more occur from people's inability to get one up in life. Each of these can be traced directly back to the repercussions of our pursuit as a species for superiority.

This same superiority complex undergirds the poisoning of our air, lakes, and waterways from the careless disposal of industrial waste due to the want of cutting costs to increase profit. It is true of our food supply as well. The insatiable desire for profit creates an environment where cattle eat while standing knee deep in their own manure as they wait their turn to be slaughtered. The resulting bacteria on their carcasses find their way not only into our meat, but also to other foods from the drainage of the same wastes into the fields that grow our crops. And not to mention the contamination from toxins in commonly used fertilizers and pesticides, all for the sake of ever-increasing production, more and more profit, and the expanded opportunity to get one up.

Our quenchless thirst for superiority also has its complications in the moral world, where humanity's conquest is not only of nature, but of each other, as well. Nearly every society has its "haves"—the nobles, and its "have-nots"—the peasants. The difference between the two is usually measured by financial worth, social status, degree of influence and power, level of education, and the sheer accumulation of better-than-average things. It is generally true that one-upmanship by the "haves" leads to their control over the "have-nots." This dynamic is more unconscious than intentional. Though it is never stated, it's as if the golden rule were to mean that "those who have the gold (the haves) make the rules (for the have-nots)."

Not to be outdone, the have-nots act out their own version of superiority. Remember, they are products of the same belief in ego separation as the "haves," and therefore play by the same rules. They simply criticize and belittle those who "have" with such labels as "intellectual snobs," "greedy bums," "uppity-ups," and the like. This is the way ego consciousness works. As water seeks its own level, egos seek ways to get or stay one up, often in the subtlest of ways, and always at the expense of others.

The I-am-superior-to-you syndrome that is deeply embedded in ego consciousness has been carried internationally to dangerous extremes. Humanity must now live in constant anxiety knowing that there are mounting numbers of weapons of mass destruction in existence which have the potential to blow the earth to smithereens at a moment's notice. There is no question that we stand on the edge of a precipice where, if ego consciousness continues to rule, our survival may be in serious jeopardy.

* * *

The situation the world is presently in has come about for very specific reasons, which is key to understanding ego. *The instinct to continue living—the survival instinct—is the most basic instinct of every form of life on earth. Based on our earliest experiences in life, we have unconsciously, and as it turns out, mistakenly, defined ourselves as separate and isolated beings. Therefore, deep in our psyche we feel that if we are to survive as individuals and as a species, this definition **itself**—that we are disconnected beings—must survive as well.*

To do so, the unconscious and relentless pursuit of one-up-manship that supports our misidentification must necessarily persist uninterrupted. Yet since all such behavior is 180 degrees removed from our true identity, the fallout can only be varying degrees of unhappiness, dissatisfaction, and suffering at all levels of human existence.

* * *

This, then, is the essence of ego consciousness. In the name of survival, we continue doing the things that support our misdirected belief as to who we think we are. We are only recently beginning to realize that these same behaviors lead to discontentment, personal suffering, and, if left unchecked, our eventual demise as a species. When you multiply one-upmanship by approximately 195 countries and over seven billion people (and growing) on the planet, how can it be otherwise than to have a world teetering on the brink of disaster?

Once we are able to get beyond the ego, we can see with crystal clarity how unnecessary all such suffering and pain is. Yet we must be cautious not to judge ego consciousness on the basis that it causes so much hurt and misery. Instead, we want to understand ego for what it is. Only then can we fully embrace it, and, as a result, move beyond it to a more peaceful and joyful place.

Chapter Nine

EGO SIGHTINGS

Ego will do whatever is necessary to survive. It uses two modes of operation to accomplish this goal. The first is to commit acts of superiority over others; the second is to perpetuate the pain and suffering that follows in the wake of all such acts. Ego doesn't care which method is operating at any given moment in time because each will lead to the same end point. The end point is validation of how we've defined ourselves as separated and disconnected beings.

This chapter is given mostly to ego's pursuit of superiority. The next chapter focuses mostly on ego's perpetuation of the resulting pain and suffering. The reason for saying "mostly" is because they run simultaneously on parallel tracks, which can make it difficult at times to distinguish one from the other.

* * *

Given that we think of ourselves as separate and disconnected beings, ego runs full throttle to get one up on others at every possible opportunity. Unconsciously we feel small, unimportant, irrelevant, worthless, nonessential, and scared. To protect ourselves, we act out behaviors that are the exact opposite—called "compensations." We act big, significant, self-important, relevant, worthy, essential, and brave—in a word, superior. Except when these behaviors are taken to an extreme, they are called "normal."

* * *

Humankind's universal quest for superiority is always relative to a particular situation and the person(s) involved in that situation. The size and the content of the superior advantage being alleged are of little significance. Listen closely and you will find that one-upmanship runs rampant, from the most menial situations to the most complex. A child stating to a playmate at recess that "I have more marbles than you do" is no less an expression of ego than a student saying to his classmate that "My score on the algebra test was higher than yours," or an executive bragging to a competitor that "We have the finest staff of dedicated employees one could possibly assemble," or the president of a country reporting to other world leaders that "We have more nuclear warheads than any other nation on Earth," or a young lad saying to the bully who picks on him at school that "My dad is tougher than your dad." Each of these cases follows the same pattern for how ego reveals itself: *I am superior to you, better than you, or one up on you in one way or another.*

The truth is that there is always someone to whom an individual can claim their superiority. One might act out behaviors that represent being smarter, bigger, prettier, or more well-read; the better athlete, musician, or typist; the more caring spouse, parent, or teacher; the most punctual, detail-oriented, or well-dressed; the best housekeeper, manager, surgeon, or painter; the wealthiest, most influential, or most powerful; the most depressed, ill, or downtrodden; or the proud owner of the biggest house, most fuel-efficient automobile, or the cutest dog. *Ego will ensure that everyone has the opportunity to act superior to someone about something.* Its game plan is always the same: strive for superiority. The details for how this is acted out can vary immensely depending on the situation and the prowess of the player(s) involved in claiming a superior advantage over the other.

* * *

To familiarize ourselves with some of the more common ways that ego manifests as a superiority complex and to recognize some of the many faces of one-upmanship, what follows is a list of "ego sightings"—behaviors where ego is clearly present. This list is not exhaustive; it's doubtful that any such list could be. It is nonetheless representative of many of the ways that ego consciousness has expressed itself throughout the course of human history and how it still plays a leading role in human endeavors to this day.

Needing to Be Right

Ego feeds on being right and making others wrong. The need to be right is the grand master of ego consciousness. When we are right we feel empowered; when wrong, we feel weak and vulnerable. Many people will go to any extreme to be right. It makes us feel superior to the other party, which is always the unconscious goal. The need to be right is how enemies are made and how much blood is shed. These consequences occur at all levels of human interaction, from petty arguments to international warfare (since countries have egos too).

The battle of right versus wrong can be fought over opinions on any issue—religious, moral, social, political, or legal; it doesn't make any difference. Everyone knows how divisive and hurtful this fight can be. At the end of the day, all that matters to ego is being right. The compulsion to be right is such an emotionally loaded issue that people who are accused of being wrong will sometimes find ways to avenge the situation. Even when one is proven wrong, one often goes away convinced that whoever made that determination doesn't know what he or she is talking about.

Becoming Attached

Because we perceive ourselves as separate and disconnected entities in the universe, it leaves us feeling insignificant and unimportant. Identifying with something and then emotionally attaching to it edifies our sense of "I"-ness. We can attach to objects, thoughts, beliefs, people—anything, for that matter. Once the attachment is made, it feels like a part of us. The more attachments we make, the more strengthened we feel. Without them we feel diminished, which is why, if need be, we are willing to fight to hold onto them.

Excessive attachment to another person, as is the case in codependent relationships, can be the result of insecurity about being alone. It protects us from feeling like separate beings in the universe. Attachment can also quickly digress to the need to be right. For example, attaching to an idea or belief automatically implies to someone who disagrees with us that they are wrong. Our propensity for passionate attachment to beliefs is why it is considered unwise to discuss religion or politics in social settings. Open disagreement or hurt feelings can easily ensue.

Projecting Blame

Whenever you project blame onto another party, you are basically saying, "You're the bad guy here; you're wrong." Of course it follows that you are in the right. It doesn't much matter what led to the spreading of blame—an incomplete project, failure to meet your expectations, breaking a rule, or perhaps just being an inconvenience for you in some way. Blame always means that the other person is wrong and you are right. It also means not accepting your own responsibility in that situation. Doing so would point the finger at yourself, which makes you at least partially wrong, and that is usually too painful to admit.

Listening to or Viewing "Negative" News

Ego thrives on "bad" news, for a variety of reasons. It creates opportunities to blame the wrongful party, which gives us a feeling of one-upmanship. It provides us with newsy tidbits to share with others, and thus the opportunity to feel one up on the person who doesn't already know. News reports of tragedy in any form can leave us feeling lucky, which is a subtle form of superiority in relation to the unlucky, who at least for the moment, are less fortunate than ourselves.

And though this is more an example of ego's second venue, it seems fitting to say here that because ego seeks suffering, one way to find it is by identifying with the suffering of others. This gives cause for many viewers to seek negative news, which the media is happy to accommodate. Doing so serves both parties well: the media makes money from increased viewership, and viewers get a steady diet of mishap and misfortune that furnishes ego the boost it needs to feel fully alive.

Gossiping

Many people love to spread sensational "facts" of a personal nature behind the back of the person being gossiped about. Some individuals are so immersed in gossiping that they become known as the "town gossip," a sort of switchboard central, especially in small communities.

At the heart of all gossip is the feeling of superiority. We feel that we are one up on the person being gossiped about, and that we're one up on the people with whom we share the juicy details: "I knew this about so-and-so, and you didn't."

Being an Authority

One of the most effective ways to counterbalance ego's feelings of unimportance and insignificance is to have an answer for everything. It doesn't always matter if the answer is correct; that would be nice, but it isn't essential.

We're all experts about something. This means that we are all knowledgeable, either through experience or formal education, on at least one specific topic. Ego-driven authority is more related to an "I-know-more-than-you" stance on just about any subject. This kind of authority relates, once again, to being right. Feeling dead-certain helps salve the chronic wound of uncertainty and insecurity that is inherent in ego consciousness.

Passing Judgment

Egos are opportunistic in grabbing every possible opening to pass judgment. Some judgments are blatantly obvious, such as: "This is your fault!" "You're stupid!" "You're wrong!" These and similar overt judgments are clear acts of one-upmanship, usually made by someone who is upset or angry. Typically the person being judged is hurt and defensive, which creates battle lines that can be difficult to repair.

Most judgments, however, are more insidious. They are made repeatedly in our everyday vocabulary. The most common examples come in the form of "should," "shouldn't," "ought," and "ought not." "You should stay more focused on your work." "You shouldn't have quit your job." "You ought to give him a piece of your mind." "You ought not talk to your children that way." Passing judgment on another person elevates the person doing the judging over the person being judged, or so it feels.

Wanting and Having

It is difficult for one's ego to be satisfied with what one has. It generally *wants* more because by identifying with material things, *having* helps one feel more important, powerful, and superior to others. For some people this turns into greed where there is an excessive or insatiable desire to acquire or possess more than they need or deserve, especially in respect to material wealth.

Participating in Drama

Many people find themselves routinely caught up in situations that involve intense conflict and emotions. Ego loves this setting because its two favorite ways of expressing itself—superiority and suffering—are happening at the same time. Typically the drama unfolds around a power struggle about who is going to have his or her way, or whose way is right and whose is wrong. Insults, criticisms, and accusations are leveled at one person or another. This invites defensiveness and resistance, and soon the fight is on. Persons close to the drama often choose sides, which escalates the emotions for all concerned. Eventually ego is satiated from such a luscious meal, the emotional fires die down, and the drama subsides until the next round, which could be hours, days, or weeks away.

Seeking Attention, Praise, or Recognition

When we receive attention or recognition, ego feels a surge of energy that says, "I am significant and count for something after all." This serves as temporary relief for how small and unimportant we feel on the inside due to defining ourselves as separate and disconnected beings. For many people attention seeking can become a way of life, where everything about them— their manner of speech, their clothing, the positions they seek, the foods they eat, the company they keep, their jewelry and other bodily adornments —all say, "Look at me!"

Acting Entitled

Entitlement is a frame of mind that says, "I have the right to be treated as someone who is more important than others." "The rules that others are required to follow don't apply to me because I'm special." Acting entitled gives one the feeling of power and superiority, both of which ego feeds on.

Having Idols and Worshipping Heroes

When trapped in ego consciousness, no matter how much we may have, in our souls we still feel like insignificant have-nots. To protect ourselves from such dreadful feelings, we try to associate in any way we can with people who are perceived as being the "haves"—even if it's only through name dropping. What one person might idolize in another can vary greatly from beauty, physique, fame, fortune, talent, or reputation to voice quality, hairdo, position power, accomplishments, or popularity. Granting people respect for their talents and accomplishments is one thing. Idolizing or worshipping anyone for any reason is another. Hero worship is ego trying to get one up by identifying with those who—at least in appearance—have already achieved that status.

Being in a Hurry

Ego loves hurrying. Insufficient time to accomplish things we want to do, even though frustrating, can—in a subtle way—make us feel quite important because important people always have a lot to do. In this frame of reference we may feel entitled to be late for an appointment, which allows us to feel more important than the person having to wait. We get to push the limits at traffic lights as they turn from yellow to red because, of course, whatever is next on our agenda is very important just as we are. Countless people are injured and killed every day at intersections around the world for this particular ego act.

Being in a perpetual hurried state also keeps our minds busy so that we don't have much time to be still and think. Ego loves this because otherwise we might pause long enough to ask ourselves, "Why am I participating in this rat race?" The answer, of course, is *because of ego*. But then, this would mean to ego that it has been discovered, and, as a result, might lose its power. In the name of survival, ego must try to keep its identity concealed.

Being Unforgiving

When people feel wronged, it is often difficult for them to forgive the other party. Partly this is because they feel hurt and victimized. But it is also true that the unwillingness to forgive puts a person in the superior position, as if to say, "You aren't worth forgiving."

Needing to Be in Control

The reason why some people need to control others is that it makes them feel empowered to get what they want out of a given situation. Feeling empowered is ego flexing its muscles and feeling one up on those being controlled.

Pushing Children to Excel

Encouraging children to do their best is different than pushing them to excel. Much of the pushing by parents is their own egos trying to keep their kids ahead of the pack so they can be one up on the others. This makes us feel more important as parents—look what *my* child has accomplished. Or, as is often the case, it compensates for what one may have failed to achieve as a child, which left wounds that never completely healed. This is why a father who felt like he wasn't recognized for his athletic talents as a youngster might push his son to become an athlete extraordinaire.

Similarly, a mother whose own parents prevented her from trying out for a high school play—something she dearly wanted to do—might insist that her daughter become an award-winning actress. The pressure this puts on children can be crippling. A secondary-school guidance counselor confided recently that she believes upward of 80 percent of the students at her campus are on drugs, both legal and illegal, just to cope with such pressure.

Advancing One's Career

Many people will do whatever it takes to climb the organizational ladder: back stabbing, sleeping with one's boss, gossiping, slandering, breaking agreements, pandering, lying, withholding information, or taking credit for another person's work. These types of behavior are commonplace in the organizational setting.

Whether on a small or large scale, all such behavior reflects full-blown ego consciousness—trying to get one up, feel superior, gain power, be recognized, become irreplaceable, and so on. In this sense an organization is an ideal example of how ego functions in the group setting. In corporations especially, this might be described as a type of "corporate schizophrenia" because it creates such a crazy environment in which to work. In truth it is the normal expression of egos when bunched together, a demolition derby of sorts in the workplace, where the goal is to beat down the other guy and try at all costs to finish on top of the heap.

Having Expectations of Others

Contractual expectations aside, expecting other people to meet your personal standards or wishes is a definite expression of ego consciousness. This is especially true when the expectations are unusually high or are not clearly articulated. In each of these cases, people are bound to fall short of doing or saying what you had hoped for, which automatically puts you in the superior position.

Being Reactive

When things don't happen the way we expect them to, we often react with feelings of frustration, disappointment, anger, annoyance, irritability, or sadness. Each of these is an emotional reaction to something being different than what we think it "should" be. "Should" is a judgment, and judgment always involves ego. In addition, these same reactive feelings are often attempts to control the situation. Where there is an attempt to control, ego is present.

Being Jealous

Jealousy and ego are playmates. Jealousy is usually expressed in relation to our other half, our partner in life. If he or she shows interest in another person, we feel the threat of being inferior to that person, as if our partner might prefer him or her to us. Much pain occurs in life over matters of jealousy. Efforts to regain superiority in the eyes of one's partner often leaves that person feeling disgusted, angry, hurt, or defensive over accusations that might have been made. Aggressive behavior toward the third party may lead to angry outbursts, fisticuffs, and even bloodshed, which can quickly translate into legal troubles. The bottom line is that jealousy is not a pretty picture, and ego loves every inch of it.

Being Envious

Envy is the painful or resentful awareness of another's advantage joined by the desire to possess that same advantage. In other words, "I can't stand the feeling that you're one up on me." "I want what you have so I can feel superior too."

* * *

Everyone exhibits different combinations of behaviors driven by ego's unquenchable thirst for superiority. Some people will act out several such behaviors; others only a few. Some may have one behavior in particular that shows itself often; others may have a variety of ego behaviors that manifest themselves relative to the situation at hand. Some will act them out with considerable animation and heated emotion; others with a poker face and few words.

Regardless, they all come from the same place and are expressions of the same thing—ego consciousness unfolding. The elements they most have in common are that they all lead either to acts of one-upmanship or incidents of unhappiness and pain. Ego doesn't have a preference, since both lead to the same place: *ongoing confirmation that the definition we've assigned to ourselves as separate beings in the world is intact and thriving.*

Chapter Ten

EGO CONSCIOUSNESS AND LIFE MAPS

In addition to ego's need to express superiority over others, there is a second venue where it works tirelessly to ensure its own survival. This is ego's propensity to attach to the painful thoughts, feelings, and experiences that linger in people's unconscious—usually since childhood—from having been subjected to superiority-related behaviors of others.

Just as our bodies have white blood cells to ward off microscopic invaders, the mind has its own armed guards, called "psychological defense mechanisms." When feelings are too difficult to cope with and too painful to remember, these defenses automatically spring into action to repress the pain from one's conscious mind. To "repress" is to unconsciously exclude painful thoughts, feelings, and memories from consciousness, which means that one is no longer aware of them. This is a common occurrence for nearly every child at one time or another in the course of growing up. Fear, anger, shame, loneliness, depression, grief, abuse, and abandonment are some of the more common emotions that are often repressed when the pain is too difficult for a child to bear.

Imagine, for instance, young Jimmy who lost his parents in a tragic automobile accident. Sally grew up with a domineering mother whom she could never please. Joe was repeatedly mocked for his slight physique. JoAnne was raped by her uncle. These are excruciatingly painful experiences. Depending on a child's threshold of tolerance for coping with emotional pain, the mind, unintentionally, might well put all such pain-related thoughts and feelings away, into the safety of the unconscious.

* * *

It would be a mistake to conclude from these examples that only the extremely dreadful pains from childhood are repressed. Very few people escape childhood without emotional scars, and therefore without some degree of repression. Those who think otherwise are likely in denial. We get our start in life as little people in a big world. We grow up in the middle of emotional fallout: parents who are often in conflict because of the stresses of marriage, careers, and raising a family, plus their own personal and unresolved emotional issues; siblings competing for attention in any way possible, which usually means doing whatever it takes to get one up on the other(s); schoolmates and friends always ready to say hurtful things; and teachers and principals who have the power and authority to reprimand in ways that can cut us deeply. Also, the emotional pain children experience need not be actually inflicted upon them. It may simply be *perceived*. But there isn't a difference. In a child's mind, perception *is* reality. Actual or perceived, emotional pain is emotional pain. Subsequently, most children's psyches become bruised—some more than others, but nearly all to some degree.

* * *

Perhaps the most distinguishing characteristic of repression—especially when it occurs in childhood—is that the repressed thoughts, feelings, and experiences don't really go away, as would appear to be the case. They go into hiding, but they are still there. The unconscious gives these thoughts, feelings, and experiences a life of their own, and in their repressed state they can actually take on power. They can—and generally do—become the "life map" that defines the direction our lives will take. They drive us in adulthood by adversely affecting our decisions, reactions, and relationships—commonly called "baggage"—which is often obvious to others, but rarely noticed by the person who carries it. When the repressed pain is "heavy," the resulting behaviors will be more obvious; when it is less weighty, the behaviors will be less obvious. But, nonetheless, they will still be there. It's just that they will show themselves in more subtle ways.

* * *

A "life map" is an unconscious emotional plan or belief system that is formed in childhood, usually by the time a child is seven to ten years of age. Although life maps can—at least in principle—follow pleasant story lines, in general they tend to be laden with repressed emotional pain.

This is because ego has an unwritten bylaw, a dictum or rule that guides its every move. *Since I survived by doing or feeling X growing up—no matter how painful—then I must keep doing or feeling X as an adult in order to feel safe and secure regarding my future.* This bylaw is the bottom line of every life map. Ego attaches to one's repressed emotional pain from childhood and then drives the behaviors in adulthood that cause this same pain to resurface and recycle over and over again.

* * *

The point was made that repressed pain in childhood is mainly caused by being on the receiving end of acts of superiority by others. Since all children in their formative years feel that their parents are superior to them—bigger and stronger with more power and authority—most of this pain comes from a child's interactions with his or her parents. This is not to say that parents intentionally act superior—or hurtful—to their children. To the contrary, the vast majority of parent-to-child interactions are well-intentioned and loving. But they are also largely role defined, and therefore are mostly spontaneous and unconscious.

As a result, parents often unknowingly create an environment where their children experience emotional pain through things said or not said, actions taken or not taken, and feelings expressed or not expressed, all in the course of daily living. However, this is not meant to imply that parents are always and only responsible for their children's emotional struggles. Instead, be reminded that pain repressed in childhood can be—and often is—greatly shaped by a child's own perceptions and interpretations of his or her experiences within the family unit during the years growing up.

* * *

Let's take a look at some actual cases—with names changed, of course, as they are throughout the book—to see how life maps can play themselves out once ego attaches to a child's repressed emotional pain.

Maggie was the youngest of four girls, ten years younger than her next older sister. As a child, she remembers her parents, relatives, and friends often commenting about how pretty her sisters were. One by one each sister grew up and left home until Maggie was the only remaining child that lived with her parents. Maggie was overweight and rather plain in her features, so she never heard any references or direct comments that she was pretty also. She tried to the best of her ability to be attractive like her sisters but never received any compliments to that effect.

One day she was playing in the yard and quite by accident overheard her mother say to a neighbor, "Maggie is such a plain-looking girl. We love her of course, but I doubt if she will ever be pretty like her sisters."

This was very painful for Maggie to hear so she tried hard to not think about it. Then one day she noticed that her fear of being ugly was gone—that it really didn't bother her like it used to. But it actually wasn't gone; it was repressed into the unconscious to relieve her emotional pain where it took on sufficient power to become her life map.

Maggie grew up, married, and had children. Throughout her entire adult life the prettiness issue deeply affected Maggie, even though she was unaware of that fact and made no connection with its source. She spent lavish sums of money on clothing and jewelry to help her feel prettier. This became a serious strain on her marriage because her husband had to work two jobs to support her spending habits. Aside from cooking meals and raising her children, Maggie spent every possible minute in front of the TV watching movies that featured glamorous actresses. She pointed out every attractive female in her view to anyone who would listen. "Isn't she pretty" were words she frequently spoke. She even dubbed one of her daughters "the pretty one," which of course her daughter adopted. But this cost the daughter dearly in her own adult life. When she gained weight and—by her own assessment—lost some of her attractive qualities, it caused much inner conflict and an extended case of serious depression.

* * *

Christopher grew up in extreme poverty. His father was an alcoholic and couldn't hold down a job. His mother was unskilled and uneducated and most of the time was unemployed. She spent much of her time crying, not knowing what to do. Christopher was upset, of course, by his mother's sadness. He wanted to help her in any way he could. Every day after school, on the weekends, and all summer long Christopher spent his time picking up bottles and cans along the highways. He would cash them in, and give the meager earnings to his mother to buy food.

Obviously this entire situation was emotionally distressing to Christopher. The sympathy he had for his mother, his own injured self-worth from not being able to fix the situation, and his fear that as an adult he too would be poor were all repressed. But, as is usually the case, that which is repressed will show up again as one's life map begins to unfurl.

In time, Christopher entered college to study finance, but soon dropped out because he discovered that he would rather get a job and earn money than spend it on his schooling. After working at menial jobs for a few years, Christopher decided he wanted to become a venture capitalist. Since no reputable firm would accept his limited credentials, he went in search of any source that would employ him. He soon fell under the spell of financial scam artists and quickly learned the tricks of the scamming game.

With a little practice, Christopher became very skilled at deceiving people and periodically made large sums of money. The long arm of the law eventually caught up with him, and he spent several years in prison before being freed. Freedom was hardly his friend, however, as he was penniless and broken in spirit. He died a few years later in utter poverty.

* * *

Lisa was an independent-minded little girl. She commonly did things that her mother instructed her not to do: play in the road, climb trees, ride her horse bareback, swim in the nearby pond by herself, and the like. Whenever her mother caught her doing something against the rules, she would yell and scream at Lisa, accusing her of being mentally retarded—stupid—and that she would never amount to anything.

The thoughts and feelings of being told she was stupid were painful, and hence they were repressed. But it wasn't long before Lisa's life map began to impinge on her everyday behavior. In secondary school she studied extremely hard to get straight A's and missed out on all the social and extracurricular activities.

Soon after graduating, she married the valedictorian of her class. With Lisa's encouragement and emotional support with regard to how brilliant he was, her husband climbed the corporate ladder quickly. When he was let go years later due to the downsizing of the company he worked for, Lisa was devastated; she secretly felt that he lost his job because maybe he wasn't as smart as she had thought.

From the time she married, Lisa had enjoyed working as a volunteer on various community projects. Typically, she would assume a leadership role in every volunteer organization she joined. This created stress in her marriage because of the late hours and frequent absences from home. She raised her children to believe that they were extraordinarily intelligent and could therefore accomplish anything they wanted to in life. When they weren't first at everything they attempted, Lisa would become very upset with them for not trying hard enough and for "wasting their lives." And God forbid anything less than an A on their report cards.

In addition, Lisa always talked as if she were an authority on all subjects because she had "done a lot of research" and therefore knew more than whomever she might be talking to about any topic being discussed. Over time, this alienated nearly every friend she ever had. This proved to Lisa that nobody liked her because—in her mind—she was stupid and never really amounted to anything after all.

* * *

Bill's parents argued nearly every day when he was young, sometimes several times a day. Their arguments were shouting matches about whatever—money, the kids, the way something was said or not said, home repairs that rarely were completed, drinking too much, you name it. The arguments were often vicious and an assault to Bill's young psyche. Many times he would go to his bedroom, hide his head in the pillows, and sob. He vowed that when he grew up he would never treat his wife the way his father treated his mother.

That vow, and the painful feelings that were attached to it, were repressed. Even though the fighting continued, Bill often found ways to be away from the house until he eventually graduated from high school and left home. He attended a technical school and became an electrician. After a couple of years he met a young lady—Lucy—who really liked him, in large part because he was so quiet and calm.

They married and in the beginning all went well. Challenges soon set in, however, because like so many couples, a close emotional bond between two people tends to cause life maps that have been lying dormant for years to surface. Lucy was the kind of person who wanted to talk about their problems. Bill on the other hand, because of his unconscious fear of arguing, was very tight-lipped. Whenever she would bring up a difficult subject, he was willing to listen but refused to talk or render an opinion. This angered Lucy, and she would occasionally yell at him for his unwillingness to deal with their issues.

Lucy thought of Bill as weak and unwilling to confront challenges. Over the years she grew tired of their lack of meaningful communication, and eventually filed for a divorce. Bill couldn't understand why his refusal to fight with her was such a big deal. To him it was a tremendous virtue. Feeling deeply hurt, Bill had a difficult time allowing himself to grow close to other women and never gained the confidence to remarry.

* * *

No doubt you noticed that each of these case scenarios ended in pain. This is the price we pay for remaining unconscious about ego's involvement in our personal story lines. Repressed pain from childhood is carried forward and shapes our life maps as adults. Ego attaches to these maps and perpetuates the repressed pain to ensure its own survival. Unless or until this dynamic is discovered by the person who unconsciously harbors it, ego will continue to cause problems in one's life, often passing the same pain from one generation to the next.

* * *

Not all life maps are caused by painful, emotional themes from childhood that resurface when we're grown. Some story lines result from thoughts and behaviors we learn early in life that repeat themselves in adulthood. Parents model ways of relating to others within the family that children can easily assimilate. These patterns become a large part of who we are as adults. When they interfere with getting our needs met in adulthood, which is often the case, we get trapped in painful behaviors that can imprison us for a lifetime.

This is where ego consciousness enters the picture. Remember, ego is focused on keeping the beliefs and behaviors alive in adulthood that we learned as children in order to survive. No matter how much pain results from these behaviors, it is of utmost importance to ego that they "keep on, keeping on," which is precisely how they can become story lines for our lives.

Several such life maps are common enough to be named. Sometimes they're referred to as "games people play." They are only games in the sense that all games follow a certain set of rules. Perhaps more descriptively, they are repetitious, painful behaviors that are difficult to break free from until we are able to see the emotional fallout they cause for ourselves and for those closest to us.

The Victim Map

Victims are people who feel perpetually subjected to oppression, hardship, or mistreatment. Many people end up as adults feeling like victims because they likely were victimized as young children by significant others in their lives.

The victim mentality is characterized in people by a pervasive "poor me" outlook, as if they can never quite get a break. Individuals who live out the victim map also feel helpless about changing their fate. This attitude is reflected in their "yes, but" response patterns whenever a suggestion is made for how they might take more control of their lives.

> "Why don't you say something to your friend when she talks to you that way?"

> "Yes, but if I do, she won't want to spend time with me anymore."

> "Then you could find other friends who would show you more respect."

> "Yes, but I don't really know how to make new friends."

> "How about joining a club where you can meet people with similar interests to your own?"

> "Yes, but I don't really have time to join a club."

And so it goes. The irony is that even in the pain that results from their own helplessness, victims get to feel quite important for always drawing the short straw. "How important I must be for bad things to always happen to me." Individuals with a victim map also tend to attract a fair amount of attention from people who feel sorry for them. Attention makes victims feel important, which is a temporary antidote for the helplessness they really feel inside.

The Guilt Map

Guilt is the feeling of remorse that occurs when we engage in some type of behavior that we believe is wrong and we therefore regret having done it (or conversely, we regret that we didn't engage in some behavior that we believe we should have). It is a feeling that is familiar to all of us, but for many people it becomes a crippling guilt mentality that plagues them for life. Guilt and shame are often thought of as synonyms. However, there is an important difference. Guilt spotlights our wrongful behavior whereas shame emphasizes what is fundamentally wrong with us. Or, as one person put it, "Guilt is what you feel when you *make* a mistake; shame is the feeling that you *are* a mistake." The first leaves us feeling remorseful for what we did or didn't do; the second leaves us feeling unworthy as human beings. For the guilt-ridden personality, both dynamics are usually at work.

The seeds for what will become an individual's guilt map in adulthood are usually sown by parents or other people in positions of authority when we were children. A child naturally wants to please its parents. However, many parents use guilt to control their children by setting standards that are difficult if not impossible to achieve. When the child falls short and fails to please its parents, it is punished for not having met their expectations. The child then feels guilty and tries harder the next time. Eventually this vicious circle leads to a guilt-ridden and shame-based mentality that permeates one's behavior in adulthood. Not only does one feel guilty for just about anything that goes wrong, one also believes that he or she isn't worthy enough to have it be any different, so why try. As with the victim map, feeling guilty much of the time can attract considerable sympathy and attention from others.

The Blame Map

When parents don't accept responsibility for their own actions, they usually blame the consequences of those actions on other people, including their own children. Mother was baking bread for dinner when her three-year-old daughter, Sara, fell and cut her head, which needed attending. When Mother returned to the oven to find the bread burned and no longer edible, she turned on her daughter and screamed, "Sara, this is your fault entirely! If you had been more careful we would have had warm bread for dinner!"

What Mother has taught her daughter is that she—Mom—isn't responsible for the results of her own behavior; Sara is. Sara also experiences that her parents blame other people for things that go wrong. It was the gas station owner's fault that Dad backed up and hit a steel post. It never should have been put there in the first place. It was the doctor's fault for going on vacation the same week that one of their sons was stricken with appendicitis. Sara will experience this same dynamic modeled by her parents over and over again in her formative years and will quite possibly "take on" this same behavior as an adult.

People who live by the blame story line are often overheard saying things like, "If it weren't for you"; "See what you made me do"; or "You got me into this." The blame map isn't a very happy place to be. People on the receiving end feel hurt and defensive. They, in turn, act out their feelings in ways that may cause heartache and suffering for the individuals who originated the blame.

The Crisis Map

Many people who grow up in crisis-filled homes learn that creating crises is apparently how the world works. It's as if things aren't normal unless there is a crisis going on. These same people are prone to carry this dynamic into their adult years based on ego's unconscious maxim: *Since crisis is the medium in which I learned to survive, then I will thrive on keeping crisis behavior alive in an attempt to ensure my survival.* This doesn't make much logical sense, but remember ego isn't about logic. It is about ensuring survival of the deeply rooted feelings and beliefs formed in the earliest experiences of life. Ego deduces that this is its best chance to continue living, regardless of the misery it causes.

The raw materials of the crisis map are exaggeration and generalization. Everything is a big deal; every problem, no matter how small, demands immediate action; everything is an emergency; and every challenge must be handled yesterday. A flood warning in one's area would mean that one's entire house will surely be washed away. The announcement that one's employer plans to lay off 5 percent of the workforce is a clear sign that the company is closing its doors. A stomachache means that one is probably developing a bleeding ulcer.

When life seems too quiet and settled, a crisis-oriented individual will create a crisis out of something that, if left alone, would prove to be of microscopic importance by comparison. Consider Betsy's mother as a case in point. Betsy is away at college and calls her parents to inform them she won't be home for the weekend as originally planned. When asked why, she reports that she just feels like staying at school. Mom alerts the campus police that something must be drastically wrong with Betsy; would they please check on her. When the police find her studying in the student lounge, they inform her parents that she's doing fine. Mom immediately calls the college's counseling services to see if they can work with Betsy to correct her "abnormal" behavior. Friends and family are alerted that something is terribly wrong with their daughter. Before long it begins to look like a circus of activity to correct something that was never a problem in the first place.

The If-Only Map

Some people grow up with parents who are always looking backward with regret. "If only I had taken a different job." "If only I had won the lottery." "If only I had studied more, I'd have graduated from college and found a higher-paying job." "If only my wife would lose thirty pounds, I'd feel better about being seen with her." "If only my husband didn't snore, I wouldn't be so tired all the time." "If only my son had better friends, I wouldn't have to worry so much about him." "If only I hadn't purchased this house, I wouldn't be so far in debt."

If we cut our teeth on if-only thinking, then chances are that we may become if-only thinkers as adults. We will never be free to enjoy the moment, never be fully contented, never understand that things happen for a reason, and never be able to look at our mistakes as learning experiences that teach us to grow and move forward. We will spend our lives wallowing in the mud of if-only thinking, long-faced and somber from dwelling on what might have been.

* * *

Remember, in order for ego to survive, it unconsciously seeks out ways for us to suffer as a means to affirm our misidentification that we are separate beings. When our life stories carry varying degrees of repressed emotions or painful patterns of learned behavior, ego needs only to attach itself to those stories to ensure its own survival. This is how life maps become the emotional drivers in adulthood. Ego takes up residence in those maps and, as a result, sets in motion a story line of repeated suffering and dissatisfaction.

Part V

Spirit Consciousness
Is the Wellspring
of Love, Joy,
and Peace of Mind

Chapter Eleven

TRANSCENDENCE

Ego consciousness is necessary in order to reach Spiritual Awareness; it is an essential stage we must pass through. This is because we can know what works only by experiencing what doesn't work, what is true by experiencing what is false, and what is real by experiencing what is not real. Once we know these things through experience (remember, experience is the teacher of all things), then and only then, we are ready for the dawning of Spiritual Awareness.

The specific path on the way to Spiritual Consciousness is different for every individual. Yet each path is lined with some variation of emotional dissatisfaction and suffering, and in that sense, everyone's journey is the same. For some this dissatisfaction and suffering is the pain of strained or broken relationships, or, perhaps, the loneliness of having no close relationships at all. Others suffer consequences from breaking the law, or social embarrassment from moral infractions. Most people experience feelings of malcontent in one form or another as the result of living out their life maps.

A common scenario in people's lives is "serial pain"—repeated suffering that results from repetitive self-defeating behaviors. This would include such things as ongoing legal violations, periodic crises, recurrent illnesses, habitual substance abuse, relationship difficulties due to recurring themes, and so on. Each instance of pain that repeats itself is an opportunity for an awakening of Spirit. Often we're not ready to take advantage of this opportunity until we experience the same misery again and again. When the mounting pain becomes too great to bear, our eyes are then ready to be opened to Spiritual light.

Until then, we remain locked in the prison of ego consciousness, which is hell. Hell is not a place; it is a state of consciousness that cripples people who are stuck in it—as the vast majority of humanity is and has been stuck throughout our history. It destroys individual lives every day and is the principal cause of emotional anguish, strained relationships, many (if not most) illnesses, poverty, greed, terrorism, and war. Collectively ego consciousness threatens to destroy mother earth and her ability to sustain us. Mostly we have become anesthetized to this fact. First it is unpleasant to think about. Second, each day that passes without incident tends to lull us into a state of forgetfulness about the horrific, yet real possibility of nuclear, biological, or chemical holocaust.

But the fact is it doesn't have to remain this way. Ego consciousness is not the end of the story. We are slaves to it only so long as we remain unconscious as to how ego functions and the grip it has held, and is still holding, on human existence. Becoming aware of ego is step one for going beyond it—for transcending it—at all levels: as individuals, couples, families, organizations, communities, nations, and as a world at large. Once this happens, we have a reasonable chance to change the course of events that would otherwise promise to destroy us.

* * *

Einstein said that the definition of insanity is doing the same thing over and over again and expecting different results. If we are to maintain some semblance of sanity, it requires doing something remarkably different. Human beings, as we all know, don't change significantly unless or until we have to. What this usually means is that we don't change until our lives become too uncomfortable or too painful to stay on the current course. It is for this reason that individuals who suffer the most from the workings of ego are often those who are the most ready to transcend it. Of course, others can do the same. It may—but not necessarily—take a bit longer, but this depends on the strength of one's will and the level of one's commitment to take the journey.

Similarly, it is the growing despair over current world conditions that promises a brighter outlook for the fate of the planet. National and global awareness is beginning to move toward the real possibility of going beyond ego and passing into the realm of Spiritual Consciousness. The sooner this happens, the greater the chance of global survival as well as increased individual well-being.

* * *

In his book *Power vs. Force*, David R. Hawkins, M.D., Ph.D., a renowned lecturer and expert on mental processes, devised a scale from 20 to 1000 to measure and describe the various levels of human consciousness. Scores under 200 represent destructive characteristics—specifically (in ascending order) shame, guilt, apathy, grief, fear, desire, anger, and pride. Scores at 200 and above symbolize constructive characteristics (also in ascending order)—courage, neutrality, willingness, acceptance, reason, love, joy, peace, and enlightenment. In the words of David R. Hawkins:[1]

> To become more conscious is the greatest gift anyone can give to the world… While the level of consciousness of mankind as a whole stood at a perilous 190 for many centuries, in the mid-1980s it suddenly jumped to the hopeful level of 207. For the first time in its history, man is now

on safe ground to continue his upward march...and this promise of new hope comes none too soon...

...[I]t's uncommon for people to move from one level of energy to another during their lifetimes. The energy field that is calibrated for an individual at birth only increases, on the average, by about five points...Nonetheless, it's possible to make sudden positive jumps, leaping up even hundreds of points. If one can truly escape the egocentric draw of sub-200 attractor fields, consciously choosing a friendly, earnest, kind, and forgiving approach to life, and eventually making charity toward others one's primary focus, higher levels can certainly be attained.

How does one truly escape the egocentric draw of the sub-200 attractor fields? It is the intent of this book to help you acquire the awareness and the ability to attain such a leap in consciousness—more precisely, a leap into Spiritual Consciousness. For this is where we find peace, love, joy, and salvation, which are the most fundamental wishes of every human being. This completion, in the end, is our purpose as a species.

Chapter Twelve

THE ESSENCE OF SPIRITUAL CONSCIOUSNESS

The attainment of pure Spiritual Consciousness is a journey. It is not something one either has or doesn't have. It is something one grows into. With each step forward, we find fewer struggles in life and more contentment and joy.

Our greatest obstacle to finding contentment and joy is not in the outside world; it is within us. That obstacle is of our own making. It is who we have mistakenly defined ourselves to be, which is called ego. We think we are isolated, separate, and disconnected beings that must do everything in our power to keep this definition of "self " alive since survival is our most basic instinct. In doing so, we unknowingly violate who we really are—beings that are connected to everything, everywhere, all the time. We are one by virtue of the fact that we all come from Spirit and are made of the same conscious "stuff."

For fear of dying, ego resists the transformation in consciousness that is necessary to move from ego awareness to Spiritual Awareness, even though this awareness is where we can experience *living* in the fullest sense of the word. Imagine a caterpillar that resists becoming a butterfly because it is afraid that it might cease to exist. That fear would obviously be unfounded because the caterpillar wouldn't really die; it would merely transform into a different, "freer" state of being.

The transformation from ego consciousness to Spirit Consciousness is much the same. It is not something to fear. Yet as much as one can "know" this to be true intellectually, the transition doesn't actually take place until one knows it experientially. Learning how to immerse oneself in this experience is exactly where we're headed next.

* * *

Once one comes to see that ego is at the core of our dissatisfaction, misery, and suffering, a common first reaction is to treat ego as an enemy that must be resisted, overthrown, crushed, killed, suppressed, or in some other way destroyed. But the desire to overcome ego *is* ego, because "overcoming" anything is one of ego's favorite tactics. So the truth is, the more you fight it, the more it persists.

Your ticket into the realm of Spiritual Consciousness is not an emotional fistfight. It is love, since love is the essence of Spirituality. Your first assignment on the path of moving beyond ego is to embrace it, not fight it. Ego is afraid it will die if you redefine yourself as a Spiritual being. "Talk" to your ego; assure it that dying isn't necessary. It needs only to transition to another state of being. Ice doesn't die to become water, and water doesn't die to become steam. They merely transform into another state.

* * *

Since you are reading this book, you may well be readying yourself to move beyond ego and make the transition to Spiritual Consciousness. Before you sow the seeds that will grow into Spiritual Awareness, it will first be necessary to till the soil to ensure the seeds take root. The best way to do this is to learn to respect your ego and thank it for all it has done for you. It has gotten you this far in life, which counts for a lot.

It would be like riding a mule up the slope of a mountain that you've decided to scale. It rains, sleets, and snows. The wind is cold and bitter. At times the mule's legs buckle from the severe elements and you fall to the ground and get bruised. Sometimes you walk beside the mule and it steps on your feet, which hurts. Then you reach the highest elevation you can attain with the help of the mule. You must make the final trek to the top of the mountain alone. At this point would it make any sense for you to say to the mule, "Look, this has been a terrible journey. I have experienced a lot of pain because of you. I hate you. Get out of my life, I never want to see you again."

It is not likely you would be so callous. You would probably pet the mule for a moment, pat it on the head, and say "Thanks for all your help. I know this has been a difficult journey for you too. But you did a great job helping me get to this point. You can rest now; I have to go on the last leg of this journey by myself. Just remember that you will always be in the back of my mind, for I know that I couldn't have done this without your help. Thank you."

This is the way you must address your ego—with love, not disdain. It has brought you this far, although with a fair amount of pain. It did its best and now you must leave it behind in order to go to the summit of your human experience. Ego consciousness is your gateway to the highest reaches of Spirit where wonderful things await you. Embrace that which has caused you much suffering. Love ego as you would love yourself, because the truth is that ego *is* yourself. It is just that you have missed the mark by mistakenly defining your "self."

* * *

The goal, then, is to go beyond the ego by moving out of the realm of ego consciousness and into the realm of Spirit. Doing so is an eight-step process. For convenience in remembering these eight steps, you need only remember the acronym LOVE LIFE, which is what happens when you move into the world of Spirit. You are loosened from the chains that have bound you to your discontentment and struggles. You are in the deepest sense of the word "free"— free from fear, free to live, and free to love.

Each letter in the expression LOVE LIFE stands for one of the eight steps. By remembering this acronym, you can easily bring to mind the step you're working on at any given moment in time. Once you get past step one, the remaining seven steps need not be followed in any particular order. Step one is like opening the curtain to begin a play: you won't get to see the play unless this is done first. After that, you certainly don't need to go through the steps in sequential order, although it is fine if you do so. They are listed as steps only because our minds tend to think in linear patterns.

It would be unrealistic to think that you can work your way through the eight steps only one time and then you're done. It is more like sailing. You don't methodically move your sails to eight different positions and then assume you will reach your destination. Instead, you must continuously adjust your sails as the wind shifts and the currents change in order to arrive at the place you want to be.

Think of the steps as being more like tools at your disposal as you proceed on your journey. Step one is the North Star that you can always rely on if it ever seems like you've lost your way. Focus on the other steps as they seem appropriate at the time. They all point in the same direction and end at the same place. After a little practice you will discover that the eight steps gradually merge into one and that focusing on any one of them is to work on all eight at the same time.

Chapter Thirteen

LOVE LIFE:
LOOK FOR EGO

Look for ego in yourself. Ego is a state of consciousness that one is unaware of when one is in it. Your initial step to move beyond ego is to find it. Become conscious of your own ego. When you are able to do so, you have, at that moment, risen above ego—gone beyond it—which automatically puts you in the realm of Spirit. You don't need to do anything at this point. Just experience your ability to be aware of ego's existence.

It will help to remember that it is possible to be conscious in different ways. For example, you could be driving a car and at any given moment be conscious of the car ahead of you, the traffic light, a billboard alongside the road, or the fact that you're feeling hungry. But you can also be driving a car and at the same time be conscious of the fact that you are driving a car.

This same principle is true in your every waking moment: *you can be conscious of you, including what you're doing, thinking, or feeling.* This is what is meant by abstraction, which is what makes you uniquely human. You can observe yourself. It is like you're out of body watching what's happening in your body. This is the level of awareness you're looking for. The goal is to know that you can notice yourself in the form of your thoughts, feelings, and behaviors. When you achieve this, you are conscious of your ego.

* * *

Looking for and taking notice of your ego is the single biggest step you will take on your journey into Spiritual Consciousness. It has similarities with learning to ride a bicycle. Someone behind you steadies the bike and you try to peddle and keep your balance at the same time. You do fine until the person behind you lets go, and then you tip over. You get up, brush yourself off, and try again. Then all of a sudden, when you're peddling along, you glance back to discover that the person who was helping you stay balanced is no longer holding on. You made it! You are free from the grip of the person who had steadied you. You still have much to learn about riding a bicycle, but you have, nevertheless, made a giant leap to a new level of freedom.

This is what happens when you learn to observe your own ego: you become freed from its grip. You are just beginning your journey and you still have much to learn about ego functioning, but you have, nonetheless, moved into a new level of consciousness. You enter a space that you probably never knew existed before. It's like having lived your entire life in the darkness and then suddenly a light comes on. You see things that you never knew were there. You will likely be surprised by all the things you are about to discover.

* * *

A common question that comes up at this point is, "How do I know what to look for?" Remember, your ego is who you think you are; who you've mistakenly defined yourself to be. You know in general what this definition is—a separate center of action, an isolated and disconnected entity in a dog-eat-dog world trying to get one up in order to survive and to succeed. But everyone has a unique version of how this unconscious quest for superiority displays itself and this is what you want to look for.

First you need to know that you can observe ego only in the present, not from your memory of something that has happened in the past. Memory is usually diluted because time and distance lend beauty to the view. So if you try to find your ego in something that has happened in the past, all you will find is your memory, not your ego.

The quickest way to find your ego is to look in situations where you start to feel upset about something. Indian mystic, philosopher, and professor Osho[1] writes: "Whenever you suffer, just try to watch and analyze, and you will find that somewhere the ego is the cause of it. And the ego goes on finding causes to suffer." For example, you may feel irritated, angry, or anxious. Feelings like these are indicators that something in your life isn't going the way ego thinks it should or the way ego expected it to be. "What is" doesn't line up with what ego thinks "ought to be." When this happens, your ego will start to squirm, whine, or scream because it's not happy with what's going on, and this causes you to feel upset. *Try not to act these feelings out, which is to be caught in ego's clutches. Instead, just notice them and be aware of what you're feeling. Doing so will give you the opportunity to notice what ego is doing. It is trying its best to make you upset.*

Each time you notice ego intruding into your thoughts, behaviors, or emotions, you are stepping directly into the world of Spirit. If you do happen to express your feelings, rather than merely notice them, you may soon thereafter find yourself asking the question, "Was that, by any chance, my ego?" The mere fact that you are aware enough to ask this question is a clear sign that the seed called "finding your ego" has just germinated. If you missed that particular opportunity to spot your ego, rest assured that many opportunities to look for it will soon follow.

There are numerous other situations when you will have the opportunity to observe your ego at work. On occasions when you notice yourself feeling or doing any of the following, ego is most certainly present:

- Feeling or acting really important
- Exaggerating a story
- Making excuses for yourself
- Blaming or criticizing someone else
- Complaining about something
- Wishing things were different
- Resenting things that did or didn't happen
- Judging yourself or other people
- Feeling like a victim, or that you have no control
- Reacting emotionally to situations that arise

The list goes on; there is no end, really. The more you look for ego functioning inside yourself, the more you will find the places it likes to hide. The key is to not judge yourself or feel that you've done something wrong when you find it. Your job is simply to look for it, notice it, observe it, and recognize not *if* ego is present in your life, but rather *where* it is hiding.

* * *

Something interesting begins to happen as you become more adept at identifying your ego: it gradually loses its emotional hold on you. Try to stay aware of this dynamic. It happens slowly at first, but each time you notice ego, the gap between ego and Spirit grows bigger. The larger this gap grows, the more Spiritual you become from the fact that you are moving increasingly into Spiritual Consciousness.

With each instance of observing ego, the more difficult it is to stay in an ego state. Ego consciousness is hell. It hurts. It is difficult and filled with sorrow and struggles. Spiritual Consciousness is freeing, patient, loving, and peaceful. It resonates with who we really are as beings: at one with all things. Once we taste its sweet nectar, we move progressively toward Spirit as if being pulled by a magnet. The further you move into Spirit, the safer you feel know-ing that you are not alone in the universe, and that you are truly secure regardless of your situation in life at any given time. You are like a submarine in that you will be traveling at depths where you are unshaken by the turbulence on the ocean's surface.

* * *

Another way you can learn to look for ego is by observing it in others and by watching behaviors that reflect their difficult emo-tions. You may see recurrent anger, manipulation, victim mental-ity, crisis orientation, selfishness, self-control issues, and more—once again, the list goes on. The more you are able to find ego in yourself, the more you will see it in others, and vice versa. One of your challenges when you find ego-driven behaviors in other people is to refrain from blaming, criticizing, or judging them even if you are doing so only in your thoughts. If you do any of these things then that is your own ego speaking.

What you are trying to do in step one of LOVE LIFE is to become aware of ego in yourself and in others. That's all, nothing more. Your goal with others, when you spot their egos expressing themselves, is to realize that they too are caught in the whirlpool of ego consciousness. This does not make them bad, indecent, im-moral, evil, or any of the other labels that are typically assigned to people for doing or saying things that are deemed unacceptable. It makes them unconscious people: unconscious of their own egos. Recognize their behavior for what it is. Know that it makes perfect sense for them to act as they do until they grow enough in Spirit to see the light *beyond* the ego, just as you are beginning to do now.

This is a crucial point to remember. The fact that you're mov-ing toward Spiritual Awareness does not make you better than those who are not yet at this point. To think so would be a clear act of one-upmanship, which is pure ego. It would be as if you're saying, "Look at me; I am superior to those people who aren't as aware as I am."

Your movement toward Spiritual Consciousness makes you more aware than many others, but not superior to them. When you were less aware than you are now becoming, you were imprisoned in ego consciousness too. If you take a moment and think about it, you will realize that you know from your own experience what an awful place that was to be. You will begin to understand the behavior of others in an entirely new and different way. You will develop compassion for them, for they know not what they do, at least not yet.

Chapter Fourteen

LOVE LIFE: OWN YOUR EGO

Owning your ego is acknowledging that it belongs to you. It is accepting the reality of your ego for what it is. It is opening yourself to a negative or uncomfortable situation that exists inside of you without attempting to protest or deny the fact of its existence.

When you first begin to observe your ego, you may not like some of the things you see. Your ego—your definition of yourself—has led you to experiences in life that no doubt were, or are, hurtful to yourself or others. You may have done or said things that you're ashamed of. Or there are things you didn't do or say that you wish you had. It can't be said enough that this does not make you a bad person; you've just been confused. You, like nearly everyone else on the planet, thought you were someone different than who you really are. Be kind to yourself and know that you've acted appropriately within the context of that confusion.

Once you learn to look at your ego without judging it, you will begin to associate ego stirrings in the present with times that ego showed itself in the past, before you became conscious of it. For example, you may notice yourself becoming irritated and want to say something hurtful to a loved one. Then it flashes through your mind that this occurred before, but you were unaware at the time what was happening. Now you know. Instead of acting this feeling out by saying something mean or disrespectful, you catch yourself observing it—noticing your ego trying to express itself in the same way—which stops it dead in its tracks. It's not that *you* stopped it; that would be your ego speaking again. It's that your awareness of ego put a stop to it. Ego is like darkness; your awareness of ego is like the light of day. When you combine darkness and light, light prevails. When you combine ego and awareness of ego (which is Spirit), Spirit prevails. It's that straightforward.

There may be occasions when you find yourself thinking about a time when your ego showed up and it was hurtful to another person. Perhaps you snapped at your spouse, yelled at your parent, or scolded your child harshly. But you didn't realize at the time how hurtful that really was to them. Then you begin to feel guilty or sorry for what you did. Given your newfound discoveries about your own ego, these feelings will probably pass fairly quickly. If they don't, then you have likely fallen back into ego consciousness. How can you know this? Because your own guilt feelings are causing you to hurt. Always remember that ego tries to impose discomfort and emotional pain in its attempts to survive. When you suffer, ego is present. Once you observe this fact—that you have slipped back into an ego state—you have, just that quickly, moved beyond the ego once again.

There may well be situations when you were under ego's spell that you now regret and you want to make an apology. When apologizing is the appropriate course of action to take—and you will know when that is—the apology itself will be freeing to your Spirit and will, therefore, help you continue moving beyond the ego into Spirit Consciousness.

* * *

Owning your ego is not just about accepting your "imperfections," your "wrongful" behaviors, or the "bad" things you've done in life. Assigning any such label to yourself is a judgment. Your ego loves to judge and you know now that where there is judgment, there is ego. If there is still any judgment left in a person's apparent acceptance of his or her ill-deeds there can never be real peace of mind. Rather, ego may be lurking in the shadows of the unconscious, waiting to find its next opportunity to surface.

Ownership is about achieving a level of awareness in which there is total understanding and acceptance that your behaviors happened in a state of ego consciousness. This is not to be construed to mean that you are making an excuse for your behavior. It's more about realizing you are not a bad person. You were simply acting out what ego wanted from you. You were not aware of how ego and its ways were expressing themselves through your thoughts, feelings, and behaviors.

As you move beyond ego by learning to watch it, everything you've ever thought, said, or done will make perfect sense. All behavior is purposeful, meaning that it makes sense given the context in which it occurs. When sailors believed the world was flat they stayed close to shore for fear of falling off the edge. When doctors believed the cause of illness was carried in a person's blood, they "bled" the person in their attempt to get rid of the disease. We could look back in history at these two examples and think, "How barbaric; they *should* have known better." Or, instead we could think, "Their behaviors made perfect sense when you consider what they thought was true at the time." The first conclusion would be ego speaking, since there is judgment involved. The second is Spirit speaking, since it is the truth.

Similarly, people who believe they are separate and disconnected beings in an alien world have little choice but to struggle to get one up on each other in order to survive. In doing so, they can't possibly avoid saying and doing things of a hurtful nature, on occasion, to other people. Is this intentional on their part? Of course not. Are people aware this is what they do? Mostly not, because it is considered "normal" behavior when operating in a state of ego consciousness.

But just as sailing close to shore and bloodletting made sense at the time, do hurtful behaviors that are born in ego consciousness make sense as well? The answer is absolutely yes when you answer after having moved beyond ego into Spirit. In that state, you own your ego and accept it without judgment for what it was at the time.

Chapter Fifteen

LOVE LIFE: VIEW YOUR EGO

There is a difference between "looking" for your ego and "viewing" it. Looking for it is learning to notice your ego in order to become aware that it exists. Viewing your ego is more like watching a movie once you've found out where it's showing.

The idea is to become a student of your ego to see how it manifests itself in every aspect of your life. Watch how it functions in relation to your significant other, with your family and friends, in your life at work, with your neighbors, with people you respect and don't respect, and with individuals you like and don't like. Relationships are a banquet to ego's insatiable appetite. Study them. They are rife with ego activity.

* * *

Everyone's ego begins with the misconception of who we are as beings: separate and disconnected entities in the world. As a result, we all must strive for superiority in order for ego to survive. But ego does not manifest itself the same way in every individual. People define themselves differently, which is their self-image, their self-worth, the identity they've attached themselves to in life.

Rarely does one have a single definition of oneself; usually one has many. These self-definitions become the medium through which ego strives for self-importance. For example, if a man were to define himself as frugal, he would likely find ways to demonstrate to others how superior he is with regard to his frugality.

Self-definitions, then, are a valuable arena in which to view your ego. Think about your own self-image and the identities you've attached yourself to in life. Then study them to see if you can discover ways that you seek superiority through those definitions. Perhaps you have defined yourself as:

beautiful	intelligent
athletic	hard working
homely	a loser
a maverick	a winner
honest	unimportant
loud	funny
hard-driving	important
dumb	dull
a lover	a fighter
a victim	weak
energetic	an entrepreneur
humble	a homemaker

There is no end. These are merely examples of identities people might take on. Usually definitions of self are socially influenced, meaning that as young people we were told that "You are this" or "You are that," and we end up believing it to be true. We accept it as a definition of who we are as individuals. The problem is that definitions limit, restrict, and confine. Attempting to live out this self-definition no matter how positive or righteous that definition may seem, means that you have to take steps—including ones that often lead to painful places—in order to *be that thing* instead of just *be*.

* * *

Let's use the case of Barbara to examine how ego had been in the middle of her own troubles. When Barbara first learned about ego consciousness, she began to look for its presence in her own life. Once she was able to identify it and own it, she was then ready to view it.

Barbara noticed that she had been told repeatedly, starting at an early age, what a wise person she was. Subsequently, she had begun to think of herself as being quite wise. Her friends would regularly come to her for advice and it was clear to her now how this had fed her ego's need to feel superior. This was her version of one-upmanship.

As Barbara replayed her own story, she remembered that she had been seriously depressed when her marriage ended. But now she could see it for what it was. She had suffered because she feared that if her marriage failed, to her it would mean that she wasn't very wise, after all. Barbara's identity—her ego—was threatened, which explained why she had endured much suffering from staying in the marriage long after it was over emotionally. When the marriage broke down, so did Barbara.

Barbara had been attached to her self-definition—"I am wise"—which was her ego speaking. Ego tends to attach itself to self-images, and then carry them to an extreme until they lead us to pain. The pain, remember, is a feedback system for ego to know that it is indeed surviving.

When Barbara was able to view how complicating and painful ego consciousness had made her life, she was free to begin learning how to simply *be*, as opposed to having to be wise. In that freedom, she was much happier and more relaxed about life. She called her trip into ego and beyond an experience of "being saved from myself."

* * *

Find your self-image and then view its story about how that led to your emotional pain. Study the probability that ego was in the driver's seat. You will find that whatever labels you've identified with and attached yourself to have caused you troubles in one way or another. This is how ego works. It carries your identity to extreme behaviors in its attempt to be superior. These extreme behaviors, in turn, lead you into suffering so ego can remind itself that it's still alive.

Learning to view your ego may lead to answers that have puzzled you throughout your life. From these discoveries will come understanding and self-acceptance, which lead to freedom, happiness, and love. These gifts lie beyond the ego. They are given by Spirit as your birthrights, but must be rediscovered after ego is exposed and you move beyond it. Beyond ego is Spirit, which to experience completely is to reach the utmost height of being human.

Chapter Sixteen

LOVE LIFE:
EXAMINE YOUR OPTIONS

The more you are able to zero in on your ego—to spot it when it flares up and study it when you find it—the freer you become from its emotional stranglehold. This is because when you become conscious of ego, it begins to recede. With each act of seeing ego at work, recognizing situations and scenarios where it rears its head, observing it before it catches hold of you, and recognizing the sore spots that ego tries to take advantage of, you put distance between ego and Spirit.

Your Spirit is like the wind that blows where it wishes. Your ego is like a giant concrete wall that blocks and disrupts Spirit from its freedom of movement. Every time you notice your ego and the misery and dissatisfaction it has caused you, you remove one more block from the wall. With the removal of each block, your Spirit Consciousness grows. The more it grows, the freer you are to be happy, contented, joyful, peaceful, and productive. With each ego sighting you move further and further away from ego consciousness and into Spiritual Awareness.

At the same time, you become more objective about things that bothered you previously. The destructive emotions that ego brought you lift like the fog in the morning sun. You have a clearer view of things. You will be surprised at how situations that troubled you in the past, no longer do.

This objectivity allows you to begin examining your decisions and actions in the stressful situations you find yourself a part of. Perhaps you've had a strained relationship with the person you report to at work. You've been frustrated by her and angry at the situation. You try to avoid contact with her in every way possible.

Then you learn about ego. You learn to look for it, own it, and view its destructive ways. You see how it has caused you much pain. You begin to notice that your ego is part of and adds to the dynamics with your manager. As you gain more awareness of your own ego dynamics in that relationship, one of two things will likely happen. The problem may go away because it dissolves in the light of your newfound Spiritual Consciousness. Or, you may become emotionally detached from the situation in ways that will allow you to make objective decisions about it. For the first time you may begin asking yourself questions that are detached from ego and therefore, also detached from painful emotions.

Might I have some responsibility in this?
If so, what is it?
Do I want to talk to my manager about it?
Do I want to change how I interact with her?
What can I do to have a more cordial relationship with her?
Could I become a better listener?
Do I owe her an apology?
Am I ready to ask for an apology from her?
Am I ready to forgive her and myself?
Is this job a fit for me?
Would I be better off finding a different job?

In the context of Spiritual Awareness, the answers to each of these questions become viable options—devoid of bitterness, anger, disgust, or resentment. You are free to choose your course of action, no longer encumbered by the weight of ego on your shoulders.

* * *

The more you are able to objectively examine your options in any given situation, the more you will find yourself able to do the same in all circumstances. Your freedom that allows for dispassionate decision making will generalize to problematic situations in all facets of your life. It will be like learning to swim. Once you get the hang of it, you aren't limited to swimming only in that specific body of water. You are free to swim anyplace you'd like.

Similarly, once you are freed from ego and move into Spirit, that freedom emanates from your soul. It translates into everything about you. It evokes an objectivity in which you are able to deal with any trouble spot in your life. It eliminates looking back and blaming. It keeps you focused on the facts of the matter in *this* situation. There are no "if onlys," "what ifs," or "yes, buts;" each of these is an example of ego stuff. Spirit will take over and an objective examination of your options will prevail.

Feeling this state of freedom is a wonderful experience. It is filled with joy and peace of mind, knowing that you are in harmony with life and that the burdens you've been carrying for so long have finally been lifted.

Perfecting this step will take a little time. Try not to be impatient. It will be akin to the rising sun in your bedroom window— just the slightest hint of light at first. But gradually the skies brighten and, in a relatively short period of time, the sun is shining through the window of your life in the fullness of its glory. Now, being in the Spirit, you are free.

Chapter Seventeen

LOVE LIFE:
LISTEN TO THE SILENCE

Spirit is quiet because it knows that silence is the loudest sound of Pure Consciousness. Ego is noisy because it engages the mind in thinking about all the troubles it brings our way. Ego noise is a constant inner chatter that we are mostly unaware of because it has always been with us. We accept it as normal.

The mind is a tool that can be useful in certain situations, but it is not necessary to use it all the time. Yet this is exactly what most people do. Ego operates on the principle that if we are thinking then we must be alive. So it rattles on incessantly from one situation or problem to the next.

Nonstop inner dialogue is tiring, just as our bodies would tire if we jumped up and down all day long. Yet our thoughts persist. Constant analyses of our own and other people's problems—things we wish we could've, would've, or should've said or done—block our glimpse of the inner peace that goes with being still.

From within the silence and stillness of the mind comes pure intelligence. This is where ideas come to us. This is where solutions are found. It is said that the only voice God speaks in, is silence. In the words of Deepak Chopra,[1] a world-renowned leader in the field of mind-body medicine and human potential, "Silence is the great teacher, and to learn its lessons you must pay attention to it. There is no substitute for the creative inspiration, knowledge, and stability that come from knowing how to contact your core of inner silence."

* * *

To be in a state of pure Spirit is to be joyful and at peace. Ego—the turbulent voice within which results from how we've mistakenly defined ourselves—is disruptive, loud, troublesome, meddling, and painful. The sound of silence is louder than ego, even when ego is screaming its loudest. When you are silent and still, ego is dormant. It has no other choice. Every act of quieting your mind will put space between your Spirit and your ego, which is the goal. In time, and with some practice, your ego will go into a permanent state of rest and you will have achieved Pure Consciousness— pure awareness of Spirit.

Silence is one of the most powerful experiences we can have as beings. It disconnects us from ego and puts us in full connection with Spirit. Additionally, being silent and still is a state of total peacefulness, relaxation, and contentment. Josho Pat Phelan,[2] Soto Zen priest and abbot of the Chapel Hill Zen Center, writes:

> I have been thinking about the relationship between stillness and contentedness. I think true contentment, is possible when the mind is still, when whatever processes we go through to create and manifest our self come to rest. In stillness, the "I want," "I think," "I feel," "my memory," "my plans," and so on stop. When wanting and thinking come to rest, the stillness and spaciousness that are left is true contentment. This stillness isn't dead space. It is vibrant and dynamic and it is what allows us to be open to the aliveness of everything else.

* * *

In order to quiet your mind, it is necessary to be in a quiet environment. Notice how ego has invaded our lives in that regard. Many people spend large amounts of time sitting in front of the TV watching programs that engage them in explosions, gunfire, or the screeching of outlandish monsters. These things hold entertainment value to those who are so inclined, but they are not the stillness needed to quiet our minds.

And it isn't just TV, or even the movies. The modern world that we live in is, in fact, a noisy place. Jets roar overhead; lawnmowers or snow blowers whir as the seasons demand; music in restaurants and department stores blare music at a decibel level that, at times, makes comfortable conversation nearly impossible.

Besides the noise that enters our ears, there is also the information assault that we experience visually every day. Ego feeds on the explosion of written information—junk mail, e-mail, newspapers, magazines, and the increasing number of hours spent surfing the World Wide Web. Having that much information around all day, every day overloads us and enhances ego's sense of security by leaving little room for the silence in which we would otherwise be able to experience our true Spiritual nature.

* * *

Do you want to quiet your ego and enter into the peacefulness of Spirit? Try walking in the woods with no talking and no technological noisemakers. Listen closely and you will hear the presence of Spirit. Sit at the beach and listen to Spirit moving gently on the waves. Turn off the TV or radio while you get ready for work in the morning or as you do the dishes after the evening meal. Listen closely, and you will hear Spirit close at hand. Find a quiet spot where you can be still and meditate. Watch your thoughts go by without attaching to them, until they are at rest and you are completely still inside. Notice the vastness and the beauty of silence. Listen for pure intelligence to speak ever so silently. Feel the peacefulness of simply being. Immerse yourself in the dance of Spirit and enjoy its innocent playfulness as it darts from star to star.

Also take note that as you go deeper into silence, ego becomes totally quiet. It doesn't need to do any of the things it normally would do: make mental noise, create acts of one-upmanship, or find ways to make us hurt—each of which is aimed at ensuring ego of its survival. In the presence of silence, you are keenly aware of being alive in the fullness of Spirit *without ego*. In that moment, ego can rest in peace. The more moments that one's mind is quiet, the more peaceful ego becomes until it rests in peace forever.

Chapter Eighteen

LOVE LIFE: INVITE CHANGE

Change is an interesting thing. We tend to resist it, and even if we do try to change, it is often difficult to accomplish. No wonder, then, that only six percent of those who set a New Year's resolution actually achieve it.

Typically, there are two motivators that drive change: consequences if you don't change and rewards if you do. Both are ego influenced because they are outer-directed; that is, they both come from outside-in. There is a third motivator of change that is inner-directed, and this type of change is powered by Spirit. On the surface all three look much alike, but at a deeper level, the differences are profound.

Ego-Driven Change (may include any or all of the following):

- ♦ Painful because of having to struggle
- ♦ Short-lived
- ♦ Makes people feel more important—the "look at me" syndrome
- ♦ Caused by inferiority complex seeking to become superior

- Results are not satisfying; awareness that something is still lacking
- Motivated by fear
- Aim is to get one up on others
- Acquisition and possession oriented
- Power-based
- Status-related
- Outer-directed/influenced by the opinion of others
- Designed to attract attention

Spirit-Motivated Change (necessarily includes all of the following):

- Relatively effortless
- Love based
- Harmonious with who we are (all one)
- Inner-directed/comes from a self-knowing
- Fearless
- Purposeful
- Lasting
- Health oriented due to respect for Spirit's temporary bodily home
- Not attention seeking
- Results are fulfilling
- Charity oriented
- Respectful of others

Most people have changes they would like to make and goals they would like to achieve. How would taking a Spirit-motivated approach differ from that of an ego-directed approach in order to effect these changes?

If the changes are ego driven, as is true the majority of the time, you would launch into your change effort and perhaps have measurable results. Yet since ego is involved it is safe to predict that, in time, the results will lead to disappointment or suffering in one way or another.

Consider the case of Max, who lost his job as a manager due to the fact that his position had been eliminated from the company. His self-esteem was bruised because he felt this was just a polite way to let him go. Being close to the age of retirement, he decided to run for an elected government office in his community rather than seek other employment. Max won the election, which for the moment salved his wound. Soon into his new position, however, Max began making decisions that exceeded his authority, unknowingly, of course, to help heal his injured self-esteem. Other city officials were offended by Max's decisions and took measures to keep his apparent thirst for power in check. As a result of his ego pushing the limits to regain his self-esteem, Max suffered even more. As the German philosopher Friedrich Neitzsche[1] said, "Whenever I climb I am followed by a dog called 'ego'."

* * *

Lasting change must be inner-directed; it must come from your Spirit rather than from your ego. Remember, you cannot kill ego. You cannot overcome, crush, conquer, or destroy it. The more you try to do so, the more it will morph into new forms and manifest in other hurtful ways. Therefore, before you attempt to make any changes, it will first be necessary to make a conscious decision to get beyond the ego and focus on becoming more Spiritually oriented.

In other words, you must first follow the steps embedded in the acronym LOVE LIFE. You *look* for your ego, *own* it, *view* it, and *examine* your options. You learn to *listen* to the silence and now you are *inviting* change into your life. Acting from your new-found Spiritual perspective you will begin to see internal changes occurring. You will become less critical, more playful, happier, more tolerant, more helpful, and more understanding. You will be more pleasant to be with, and more watchful of your language so as not to offend others. You will become more attentive to your health and wellness. Things that used to bother you will seem small by comparison. You will see things in your own behavior and in the behavior of others that you may not have noticed before.

With all these positive changes taking place, you will find yourself inviting other changes that you desire into your life. It won't frighten you due to fear of the unknown. You will gain the confidence of knowing that the changes you seek will come from the inside out, from the purity of Spirit. You will know all such change will be void of ego and grounded in love. None of these changes will happen because of any extreme effort on your part. They will happen naturally over time because they are in alignment with your Spirit. If you remember to periodically *invite* Spirit-related changes into your life, they will happen even sooner.

Chapter Nineteen

LOVE LIFE: FEEL THE MOMENT

It is conventional to think of time in terms of past, present, and future. When you take a closer look you will see that what we call "past" is available to us only in memory, and all thoughts from memory can be experienced only in the present. For example, suppose that you are thinking about a time last week when you had lunch with a friend. That thought is a memory and memory is a present experience, something that is happening now.

Similarly, what we call "future" is available to us only by way of anticipation and projection, which, again, we can experience only in the present moment. For instance, suppose you are thinking about a movie you plan to attend this coming weekend. That experience doesn't exist in the future; it exists *now* as anticipation. Every thought you might have about the upcoming movie can exist only in the *now*. Neither would it prove that the future does, in fact, exist if you exclaim when you finally arrive, "See, there was a future after all." For being at the theater, like all experiences, exists only in the *now* at the time it occurs.

The *now* is all there is, was, or ever could be. It is eternal. Past and future are merely conveniences that serve a practical purpose in our daily affairs. Surely it is advantageous to make allowances for next week's groceries or next month's rent. And without clocks and calendars it would be impossible to agree to meet at a certain time and place, or to know when to start and stop working at your job each day.

The problem is that ego enters the picture and puts its own spin on the meaning of time. Remember, ego believes that we are separate visitors in an external and unfriendly world. Based on its own sensation of separateness, ego quite naturally separates itself from other, "I" from universe, soul from body, and "me" from "my experience." *This separation of "me" from "my experience" is where the illusion of time—the notion that there is a past, present, and future—clouds our awareness of the reality of time—that now is all there is.*

The point is that ego consciousness is time-bound. We live in the anxiety of resenting things that didn't happen in the past that we think should have happened and regretting things that did happen in the past that we wish hadn't. We worry ourselves sick about the "what ifs" of the future. "What if I get cancer?" "What if I don't make enough money to put my children through college?" "What if I lose my job?" "What if I end up a homeless person living on the street?" Given our preoccupation with a past and a future that doesn't exist except to the extent that ego promotes it, the present for the vast majority of people is a hodgepodge of painful memories and anxiety-ridden anticipations.

* * *

You will recall that in the first step of LOVE LIFE—the first L—we were working on ways to "look for ego." This notion that there is a past and future presents us with another clue for how to identify ego as we travel the path to get beyond it. If you can identify any distress in your life based on something that occurred in the past or something that you fear might happen in the future, then you know unequivocally that you've found another place where ego likes to hide. Every time you recognize your ego at work when you feel stressed about past or future events, it is one more step forward in neutralizing ego's hurtful ways.

* * *

Humankind strives for eternal life, but seldom do we know that eternal life is *now*. Spirit knows that the *now* is all there is. It knows its home is the *now* and that the *now* is the only thing that is eternal. We are accustomed to think of eternal as being forever, but perhaps the expression *now-ever* comes closer to what eternal really means. And we are in touch with *now-ever* whenever we are fully present. David R. Hawkins,[1] M.D., Ph.D., writes, "... Presence is silent and conveys a state of peace. It's infinitely gentle and yet like a rock. With it, all fear disappears, and [S]piritual joy occurs on a quiet level of inexplicable ecstasy. Because the experience of time stops, there's no apprehension, regret, pain, or anticipation. The source of joy is unending and ever-present."

* * *

Ego is fraught with problems. It tries to capture your attention every waking hour of the day, which can make it difficult to stay in the moment. This is the reason why many people arrange to take their vacations at quiet places—cabins in the country, cottages by the sea, campsites along the river—to be close to nature. These settings simulate a meditative state where ego is quiet and you're able to be fully present, at one with Spirit in the eternal *now*.

As you become increasingly aware of Spirit operating in your life, you will begin to experience the presence of the moment no matter where you are or what you're doing. Spirit is always home because it can't be anywhere *but* in the present. *Spirit is the present*. The secret is to become conscious of this fact by continuously experiencing the moment. As you learn to do so, you will grow in the awareness that you already are, always have been, and always will be in the eternal *now-ever*.

Chapter Twenty

LOVE LIFE:
EXPRESS YOUR LOVE

The essence of Spirit Consciousness, which is Pure Consciousness, is love. Yet love can mean so many different things. The English language, for example, has more than twenty definitions of "love" in an average-sized dictionary.

Many languages use fewer words for love, and each is very specific to its application. In Greek, for instance, there are five such words. "Agape" means having a general affection, such as "I love to work in my garden." "Eros" is passionate love, including sensual desire and longing. "Philia" is brotherly love and includes loyalty to friends, family, and community. "Storge" means a natural affection that is used almost exclusively as a way to describe relationships within the family. "Thelema" is the desire to do something, such as "I'd love to be a professional dancer."

Spirit love is not any of these definitions by itself, and it is more than all of them put together. It is pure love, and pure love means the absence of ego. Ego blocks the expression of pure love that flows naturally from Spirit, just as clouds can block light that flows naturally from the sun. Remove the clouds and you have pure sunshine; remove ego and you have pure love. It is that simple. We must remain aware, though, that ego isn't removed by condemning it or beating it up. Ego goes away on its own as you become increasingly more conscious of it.

* * *

Ego's premise is that people must fend for themselves if they hope to survive. So ego by nature is *self*ish. It acts according to the principle of one-upmanship. Its golden rule is to "do unto others before they do unto you." Ego always puts itself at the center and tries to get everything and everyone to orbit around it.

What remains when ego dissipates is pure love, Spirit love, which is all possible definitions of love rolled into one. Ego love is not pure. It always has a selfish motive, no matter how innocent and altruistic its presence may look to an observer. Ego love is like "fool's gold," which is pyrite, a mineral of little value that is similar in color and shape to gold. In the heyday of mining it was often confused for the real thing because of its striking resemblance. Similarly, ego love masquerades as pure love, but they are decidedly different things.

Ego love requires that there be rules and regulations to govern it. Since it always operates with "me" in mind, it will inevitably become hurtful to others because people become little more than means to ego's ends. Spirit love needs no rules because, with ego gone, it is pure. The "I" is missing and love will always manifest in benevolent and charitable ways. Pure love has its own intelligence and knows precisely how to reveal itself, depending on the nature of the situation. It is never improper and will express itself to everyone including partner, children, colleagues, family, neighbors, friends, community, or country, and to all inanimate objects, plants, animals, and all other human beings.

* * *

Some people are concerned that if ego is removed from the picture, then love becomes passive and will cease to flow. Since ego doesn't benefit, why bother to express love at all? Notice that this question is ego influenced: it makes sense only when viewed from within the perspective of ego consciousness. Essentially, it is asking, "What's in it for me to express love if I don't gain from doing so?"

From the perspective of Spirit this is never a concern, for two reasons. First, Spirit love is active. It is always on the lookout for ways to express itself. It is charitable in nature and has the best interest of everyone in mind. It is kind and forgiving, understanding and wise, helpful and earnest, genuine and respectful, gentle and honest, gracious and amiable, courteous and fair. It is all of these attributes and more. And in the end these characteristics of love really aren't different. They are each expressions of the same pure love wrapped in different-shaped packages.

Second, Spirit love does not seek attention or wish for positive feedback. Pure love is given because its nature is to give. Birds don't seek praise for the songs they sing; that's just what they do. The sun doesn't wait to be thanked for lighting and warming the earth; that's just what it does. Spirit needs no praise for loving; that's just what Spirit does. It loves unconditionally, which is the purest form of love there is.

The further you move beyond the ego, the more you will be filled with pure love. Express that love freely. Don't hold it back, but then, this doesn't really need to be said. Once you are free from ego, you can't really restrain your love if you try.

Chapter Twenty-One

LIFE IN THE SPIRIT

To live fully in the Spirit is to live in harmony, peace of mind, and love. To live fully in ego is to live in disappointment, anxiety, and suffering. When you begin moving from ego consciousness to Spirit Consciousness, it would be very unusual to make that leap in a single bound. You may experience a feeling of exhilaration that *seems* like you've just made such a leap when you first discover and begin to learn how your ego works. This is because you've just entered a new dimension of consciousness that promises to free your Spirit, which is energizing, and you are eager to learn all you can about it.

You will need to keep in mind that in order to move *beyond* the ego, you must first move *through* it. Ego is the unconscious total of how you've defined yourself, which starts with feeling like a disconnected being in the world. Even though that definition has led you to internal anguish and external conflict, it has nevertheless gotten you this far in life and it doesn't want to die. It acts like a sleeping dog: harmless until something awakens it, and then it will suddenly bark, growl, and even bite, if necessary. It is the same with ego. Old thoughts, feelings, and behaviors that were painful before you started your journey can return just when you begin to think that perhaps you are free of them.

In actuality, there will be some days when you feel *on* and you can clearly see that ego is diminishing. There will be other days when you feel *off,* which means that for the moment ego has regained some control. This is normal. When it happens, try not to pass judgment with thoughts like "I'm no good at this," "This isn't working," or "Should I even try to keep going?" Avoid if possible beating up on yourself because whenever you do so your self-criticism is the next act of ego expressing itself. If you become anxious about getting beyond your ego and you want it to go away immediately, this anxiety is your ego showing itself yet again.

This is why you can't be impatient. When you push the process and try to hurry it along, all you do is prolong it. Instead, just watch your ego and know that you are making steady progress every time you can identify its presence. Be patient and don't be in a hurry. Look for ego, view it, study it, and grow to understand it. Then one day you will look and you will no longer find your ego. Things that upset you in the past seem inconsequential now. This is when ego has been dropped. As if by magic, it will be gone.

In the meantime, if you feel it is important to measure the progress you're making on your journey, think of ego presence in terms of "frequency," "intensity," and "duration." Frequency has to do with how often ego resurfaces; intensity with how vivid the feelings are; and duration with how long the ego attack lasts. As ego manifests itself less frequently, as the suffering it causes becomes less intense, and as the ego-induced pain persists for shorter and shorter periods of time, then you can be assured that your ego is waning—inch by inch and ounce by ounce. But remember, you cannot force ego to show up less frequently, you cannot mandate that its pain is less intense, and you cannot make it last for shorter periods of time. Trying to do any of these things would, again, be to prod ego with your intent of overcoming it. Doing this would only feed ego an energy bar. The result will be that you've actually energized it to return again to fight.

* * *

In between ego episodes and as ego gradually recedes, you will likely begin to notice some remarkable, yet subtle changes in your life. It is not as if there are dramatic changes on the exterior of your life—you won't change from a simple peasant to a knight in shining armor. It is more that you will see things differently and experience life in a qualitatively different way. There's an old Zen proverb to this effect. A Zen Master was asked how his life had changed when he became enlightened. He replied, "Well, before enlightenment, I carried water and chopped wood. After I became enlightened, I carry water and chop wood." In other words, your tasks and responsibilities don't change, but the perspective you bring to those tasks changes immensely.

Here's a real-life example. A husband and wife reached an agreement that she would prepare the evening meals and afterward he would wash the dishes. Before he began his journey through and beyond the ego, he found washing the dishes to be a tedious job that he dreaded doing every night. After he became a student of the Spirit, this all changed. He began to see his responsibility for doing the dishes as a Spiritual experience. It was a renewal and cleansing that symbolized his own renewal and cleansing for every time he identified ego and discovered its ways.

Please note that this gentleman's transformation was not because he changed his attitude. Attitudinal change is related to trying to look at something differently—to see it without judgment. This kind of change is usually short-lived because it tends to address the symptoms of the problem—the behavior—rather than addressing the problem itself—ego. Real change—change that endures—results from self-awareness, which quite literally means becoming aware of one's "self," or ego. When you become aware of your ego, it loses its supremacy in your life. It is like the monster in the dark that your child is afraid of; it disappears altogether when you turn on the light.

* * *

Changes due to a growing awareness of Spirit are internal. They happen from the inside out. It would be difficult to enumerate all such changes for two reasons. First, the list would be tediously long; second, many of the changes are unique to each individual. Nevertheless, there are some generalities about the kinds of changes that usually occur, not necessarily to the same degree in every individual, but to some degree in nearly everyone. These changes happen over time, as follows:

> You become more aware of how ego influences what people do and say. You see that the struggles people experience in life are the result of their own ego functions. You are more compassionate toward them because you know that their "negative" behaviors are actually the consequence of being unconscious of their own ego. And you see that this is not a fault, but rather, a fact—one that you know all too well from the struggles you've had with your own ego over the years.

> You are more open with others, friendlier, and genuinely more loving and caring because you understand human behavior at a much deeper level. You are able to identify hurtful behavior for what it is because you've gained more insight into the fact that it is one's ego that makes one behave in hurtful ways.

> You exhibit a level of personal morality and ethics that you may have strived for in the past, but found difficult to achieve. Now you "do unto others, as you would have them do unto you" because you choose to, not because you think you *should.* And you know how to express this principle actively and appropriately because it is the nature of Spirit to do so.

➤ You become more in tune and cooperative with the natural intelligence of your body, which knows exactly what it needs to be healthy. Ego gets in the way of hearing the messages our bodies send us. Freeing yourself from ego allows you to be more attuned to your body, and to treat it as the temple—the temporary home of your Spirit—that it really is.

➤ You find yourself being less critical and judgmental, and more open to loving and accepting what is. Passing judgment is one of ego's favorite pastimes. It makes us feel important to think we are able to discern what people should and shouldn't do, what the weather should or shouldn't be, and what should or shouldn't be different at any given moment other than what is. You come to discover in the bigger picture of life that no one knows what is best or not, and what should or shouldn't be. You develop a much more calm, patient, and relaxed point of view—"Instead of judging X, let's just wait and see."

There is a Taoist story of an old Chinese farmer that speaks to this point. He had worked his crops for many years. One day his only horse broke out of the corral and ran away. Upon hearing the news, his neighbors came rushing over. "Such bad luck," they said sympathetically. "Maybe," the farmer replied. The next morning the horse returned, bringing with it two prize wild horses. "How wonderful," the neighbors exclaimed. "Maybe," replied the old man. The following day, his son tried to ride one of the untamed horses, was thrown, and broke his leg. The neighbors again came to offer their sympathy on his misfortune. "Maybe," answered the farmer. The day after, military officials came to the village to draft young men into the army. Seeing that the boy's leg was broken, they passed the farmer's son by. The neighbors congratulated the farmer on how well things had turned out. "Maybe," said the farmer.

Beyond the ego, many of the absolutes in your life turn into maybes. You don't get as upset over little things because you are more appreciative of what is as opposed to what you think things ought to be. Ego thinks it always knows right from wrong, good from bad, and should from should not. Spirit is wiser and knows that only ego thinks this to be so.

➢ You experience more joy and less sorrow, not because of increased successes and fewer failures, but for the sake of joy itself. Joy is Spirit's natural state. Everyone wants to be happy and people strive to achieve it every day. But there is a maxim called the hedonistic paradox, which states that "the more actively you seek out happiness, the less likely you are to find it." The secret to being happy, then, is to experience the joy that comes with a receding ego. Happiness is merely a by-product of Spiritual joy.

➢ You aren't as attached to beliefs, ideas, things, or people. This doesn't mean that you don't honor your beliefs and you aren't close to your loved ones. It means that you aren't dependent on them for your well-being. Ego seeks attachment; Spirit does not. Ego builds codependent relationships, which is the source of much emotional pain. Spirit is free and doesn't know the meaning of this kind of attachment.

➢ You sense your connection with all things. You know beyond the bounds of logic that birds, flowers, weeds, rocks, tables, clouds, animals, people, the moon, and the stars are all made of the same conscious "stuff." You are they, and they are you. You *love life* and all that is in it—everything, regardless of whether ego calls it good, bad, or indifferent.

➤ You notice that you have no need to continue trying to be one up on other people. Your security doesn't come from making it to the top of the heap; it comes as a result of realizing that you are an inseparable part *of* the heap. Life is no longer you against the world by striving to be better, smarter, more educated, stronger, wealthier, or having a more sophisticated title than the next guy. Life becomes all for one and one for all. You begin seeking out ways to lighten other people's loads instead of trying to be superior to them.

➤ You don't crave and unconsciously solicit strokes from other people about how important you are. The need to feel important is a sign that ego is stirring. This doesn't mean that you don't appreciate being acknowledged for a job well done or enjoy other compliments that are a normal part of social exchange. Egoistic attention seeking is a different matter. It is ego saying "I need a shot of one-upmanship to dull the pain of feeling so unimportant." On your journey to get beyond the ego, you begin noticing even the subtlest ways your ego seeks attention. When you get to this point, that need may extinguish fairly quickly.

➤ You don't get upset if someone says or does something to you that in the past would have felt hurtful. Once you discover your own ego and study how it works, you can easily spot ego in others. You know now how much others must be suffering from their own egos in order to behave in hurtful ways toward you. For this reason you are more forgiving. You realize when people are unconscious of their own egos that it is through no fault of their own. You forgive them because you are aware that they know not what they do. The love that fills you as your own ego continues to diminish reaches out to the suffering of others who would be hurtful toward you.

➢ You understand your own life map(s) better and why they have caused you such suffering over the years. Life maps can, at first, be slippery to get a handle on because they've become such a fundamental part of who you are. In many cases, they can actually dominate your personality. There is much to learn about life maps and how they've influenced your own life. Knowing this, you become quite skilled at watching, studying, and learning about ego's involvement in your personal story line. You find yourself becoming more proficient at identifying situations where ego is acting out—or perhaps more accurately—acting up.

➢ You are more productive, but for a different reason than in the past. Ego can be the driving force behind much productivity because it thrives on the accumulation of wealth and power, overcoming challenges, and being recognized for achievement. However, it is not uncommon for productivity attributed to ego to have physical and emotional repercussions—strained relationships at work and at home, disproportionate greed, physical and emotional health problems, loss of sleep, and others like these. Once you get beyond the ego, your productivity is the result of the energy you feel for life and the joy you find in your work. You see your job in a different light. The collective energy that results from the compassion you have for other people draws out a more cooperative effort from all concerned.

➢ You become less reactive to situations that might have upset you in the past. You understand that if something was troubling to you, then it was your ego speaking at the time. Rather than react in anger, frustration, or dismay you come to identify that the problem was *not* the situation you were in: it was an attack by your ego in reaction *to* the situation. Every time you can spot ego in the middle of your reactivity, you are that much closer to ego losing all control it may have had over your feelings.

➢ There is a spot in your heart that wants to make amends with anyone you think you've offended or hurt in life because of the actions of your ego. This feeling is very common as your journey into Spirit progresses. You see very clearly now that ego was a big part of what caused the hurt. You look back and remember how much you felt in the right, at the time, for your offending words or actions, and how wrong the other party was. Now you see that this was not true at all. You were not right and they were not wrong. You had an ego clash, and by your own ego's assessment, you won. At the time that felt totally justified. Now you regret it, but in short order you remember that regret is another ego event. When you identify that this is the case, your regret turns to warmth that wants to reconcile the situation. Wherever, whenever, and however it is appropriate to do so, you will.

➢ You live in the moment and see the wisdom, beauty, and intelligence in all things. You realize that the present is all there is. Life is a series of never-ending *nows*, and to be fully alive is to live each *now* as it comes to you. In this state of consciousness you are in tune with what is—not just at *any* given moment, but at *every* given moment. You are more attentive to whatever you're doing. If you're mowing the lawn, you mow the lawn. If you're making the bed, you make the bed. If you're listening to your spouse, you listen to your spouse. You are there fully, wherever you are. You accept and love what is rather than fight it because otherwise, you know that ego is in charge.

➤ If you were extroverted while under the influence of ego, you become quieter, listen closer, and don't need to attract as much attention as you did in the past. If you were more introverted before, you are likely more outgoing and friendly with people now. You not only understand yourself and others better, you also feel joy in your heart. You experience love as active and wanting to express itself. Connections with people simply become easier.

➤ You have more energy. You may even find that you require less sleep. Life is waiting to be lived and you are more excited about living it. Spirit love is active, energetic, and looking for ways to express itself. Your excitement is not a manic-like state of hyperactivity. It is an energy that fills you with a sense of well-being, peacefulness, and clarity of thought. In that frame of mind your energy will be expressed appropriately, even if it's just a smile or a wave to another individual that exudes your heartfelt love and joy for living, or as a charitable act to a person or a cause.

➤ You are less prone to worry. When all is well in your inner state, outer things are less troublesome. Worry is always about past or future events. But past and future exist only *now*. So to be—and stay—in touch with the present moment is to set worry on the shelf. It isn't needed any longer. Wherever there is worry, ego is present also. When you are able to observe in yourself that ego is at the core of your worries, you've neutralized it in that moment and added more distance between your ego and your Spirit. The result is a clear-headedness that allows you to make wise decisions and to pursue the most appropriate courses of action.

➤ You become more adept at using facts rather than judgments when you have a concern that involves other people. When the man you've hired to paint the interior of your house spills paint on the carpet, ego would say something like, "You incompetent fool! What a mistake I made by hiring you! This is going to cost you big time!" Now that your ego is still and you're in a state of Spiritual Awareness, you stay within the facts and refrain from judgment or criticism. "I see that some paint spilled on the carpet, and I'm sure you didn't mean for this to happen. We need to figure out what to do about it. What do you see as our options?"

* * *

Your journey from ego to Spirit is just that—a journey. Life in the Spirit is not a matter of being completely beyond ego in order to enjoy the fruits of Spiritual Consciousness. It isn't that simple. Growing in Spirit is a gradual process. The key to remember is that *well begun is half done*. The rewards in the beginning are so striking for most people that Spirit draws us and urges us to continue on, knowing there are many rewards yet to come. Still, you must be patient and persistent until ego lets go completely. It will hang on as long as possible until it knows you will be okay without it.

Chapter Twenty-Two

INTERPRETATION AND SPIRIT

As the band played the school song at the conclusion of a pep rally for the upcoming soccer game, the soccer team stood up and left the auditorium single file. One observer said to another, "What a nice way to honor the team." The other person was aghast and said, "How rude of those soccer players to leave while their school song was played!"

* * *

An extended family was gathered around the table for a Thanksgiving dinner. During the meal, they discussed the news about a man who was recently arrested for running nude down the main street in their small town. Grandpa said, "I never did trust that man. He's just plain crazy!" Grandma responded earnestly, "Now, Grandpa, don't be so mean. He couldn't help it. The poor fellow's suspenders must have broken and his pants fell down."

* * *

A couple had planned to send their daughter to public school when she turned five years old. At the last minute, they decided to home school her instead. The neighbors that lived on one side of them reinforced the parents' decision on the grounds that public schools are no longer safe environments for children. The neighbors on the other side criticized them for preventing their daughter from becoming properly socialized through interactions with other children her own age.

* * *

In each of these cases, both parties had access to the same facts, yet each reached a different conclusion. How does this happen?

The answer is that every individual adds his or her own interpretation to a given situation. To "interpret" means to conceive of some object, event, or person through the view of one's own beliefs or experiences. In effect, interpretation construes or translates the meaning of something after it passes through an individual's mental and emotional filters, which differ significantly from one person to the next.

On the surface this seems innocent enough. After all, what difference does it make that people have different interpretations of the same thing? In the examples used so far, it probably doesn't matter all that much. There are instances, though, where interpretation *does* matter. And the biggest such instance is when ego enters the picture via our life maps.

Interpretation connects with ego when one's ego becomes the main screening device through which one takes in information. If ego is not present in one's filter, one experiences X and then thinks or feels X. But when ego *is* hiding in one's filter, one experiences X, but then thinks or feels Y. In other words, *one of ego's preferred ways to create suffering is to distort the perception of reality by funneling information through a filter that is dense with childhood pain.* The result is a skewed interpretation of reality that is laced with hurt and suffering.

* * *

Here is an adult male—Mike—who was raised in an environment where his father was extremely jealous of his mother. There were innumerable arguments due to Mike's father suspecting his mother of infidelity. Mike was emotionally traumatized early in life by his parents' vicious quarrels. Unknowingly, Mike repressed the memories and emotions related to his father's jealousy and his mother's defensiveness.

Mike grew up and married. One year later they gave birth to a daughter. Aside from the usual adjustments of having a newborn in the home, things went relatively well. Two years after having their daughter, they had a son. Soon afterward, Mike grew increasingly agitated. He interpreted his wife's attention toward their son as preferring the child to him. Mike experienced X (his wife's love for their son), but felt Y (she prefers our son—another significant male in her life—to me). Acting from his own unconscious jealousy, Mike shunned his son and was emotionally absent from him throughout his son's formative years. Mike and his wife experienced much controversy over this issue, resulting in considerable unhappiness in the home.

Their troubles were complicated further when Mike was diagnosed with multiple sclerosis and his wife had to begin working to support the family. Every evening when she returned home, Mike quizzed her about which men she had talked to that day and pressed her for every word that had been spoken between them. Then he would berate the man in question, lecture his wife that the only motive the man had for talking was to start an affair, and demand that she never speak with him again. God forbid if she were more than fifteen minutes late arriving home from work. Mike's interpretation of her tardiness was that she must surely be involved with another man. This was usually so traumatic for Mike that he would lapse into an emotional meltdown until he was exhausted.

Mike and his family were miserable from the periodic bouts of jealousy, which persisted for years. Keep in mind that *ego relies in large part on misery to survive*. In this case, ego thrived on at least two generations of pain—Mike's and his father's. If the truth were known, this same jealousy likely existed in several generations before Mike and, if it remains unconscious, may well be passed down through several more. This is because ego hides in the filters through which we take in information, and then distorts that information in ways that make us hurt. In precisely this way, ego *utilizes interpretation to ensure its own survival from one generation to the next.*

* * *

Ego utilizes life maps to assert itself through interpretation. "Victims" interpret situations that happen in their lives as proof that they are helpless individuals. People with "guilt" maps interpret everything that goes awry as being their fault. The "blame" story line interprets that other people are at fault when things don't go as planned. The "crisis" map is highly reactive to situations because it interprets even the slightest problem as urgent.

As an example, suppose a young woman in her early twenties, Erin, decides to drop out of college and join the military. How might this situation be interpreted by different people—let's say each is her mother—according to their own life maps?

- The Victim life map: "That's my daughter for you; she's joining the military to hurt me, just like she always does."

- The Guilt life map: "I'm sure it's my fault; I guess I haven't been there for Erin as a mother."

- The Blame life map: "You can blame her father for this one; he never did want Erin to go to college."

- The Crisis life map: "I don't know what I'm going to do! Just as sure as anything, she's going to be shipped overseas and get herself killed! I've got to hurry and talk her out of this before she destroys her life!"

All difficulties that come from one's life map are a function of ego distorting one's interpretation of reality. Reality, as it relates to Erin, was that she wanted to leave college and join the military, nothing more.

* * *

In order to move beyond the ego and into Spirit Consciousness, it is important that you become adept at identifying and understanding your own life map(s). When you are able to do so, you will begin to notice how situations that caused you pain in the past were actually skewed by your interpretation of the situation. By understanding and observing your ego at work in the way you interpret things, ego will gradually diminish, along with the pain that is attached to it.

Remember, ego is highly active in close relationships. This is where ego was born, so this is what it will cling to the tightest in its attempt to survive. Relationships are often the last bastion for ego to do its work, and therefore may be the last place where it is willing to let go. Knowing this, relationships can be rich hunting grounds to look for and study how your ego functions.

* * *

To move into Spirit by identifying and isolating ego in your life map(s), there are four steps that many people find helpful. These steps are especially useful when one's map clashes with the life map of another. If you have a significant other and you're experiencing unhappiness in your relationship, then consider doing the following:

1. Identify the sore spots in your connection together because this is surely where your respective life maps

are painfully entangled and where ego is working in *both* of you. It is never just one person who is totally responsible for the conflict; it is always split 50-50, no matter how it may seem. So try not to blame each other. Blaming and judging feed ego by stirring up more suffering.

2. Each of you separately must try to identify your own life map. Trace your respective hurts as far back as possible to see how the same situation that causes you pain now might have been happening in your childhood. Ask yourself the question, "What did I wish for when I felt hurt as a child that would have made it feel better?" Whatever you discover is the answer to this question may be exactly what you wish for from your significant other now. When your wish isn't fulfilled by your partner you hurt deeply while ego celebrates.

3. Begin to discuss as dispassionately as possible how your two life maps get tangled up with each other. From there, you can work together to find ways to help heal each other's wounds. Learn to say, "When such and such a situation happens, I hurt a lot. Can you help me with that?" You will find that the further along each of you are on your respective journeys, the more you're able to share your hurts with one another. The more you can share the source of your suffering, the more help you can be to each other.

4. Try to avoid interpreting those situations that seem to be causing you the most hurt. Instead, describe as factually as possible exactly what was happening immediately prior to your feeling hurt and then what change led to you feeling upset. Staying with the

facts prevents interpretation, which minimizes ego's involvement and reduces the pain.

For example, the facts regarding the woman who dropped out of college to join the military are just that: she decided to leave college and join the military. Acting from Spirit Consciousness, a concerned mother might respond by saying to her daughter, "I don't fully understand why you decided to do this. I'd like it if you could help me to understand better. The bottom line is that I respect your decision and will do whatever I can to help if this is what you really want to do."

In the case of Mike and the jealousy he feels toward his wife, he might practice stating the reality of the situation without adding his own interpretation. When his wife is late, first he would notice his anxiety and be aware that his ego is present. Just that awareness alone may calm Mike enough to be able to say, "I notice that you're home later than usual." Assuming Mike has identified his sore spot related to jealousy and has shared it with his wife, he can then say something similar to, "I'm feeling really anxious about where you've been. Can you help me by sharing what held you up?" The other half of the problem is that his wife's parents yelled at her frequently as a child. Her life map was to become silent and close down emotionally whenever Mike raised his voice toward her, and this is where their two story lines became painfully entangled. When Mike yelled at her she would clam up, which inflamed Mike because he interpreted her silence as an unwillingness to admit to an affair. Again assuming she has shared this hurt with Mike, she could say, "Yes, I will talk to you about why I'm late, so long as you don't yell at me. When you raise your voice, I become frightened and I can't remember what I was going to say, so I don't say anything."

The secret is to stay with the facts. Doing so removes the emotion that ego rides like a bucking bronco, stirring up as much trouble as possible.

* * *

When you're in the middle of pain, carrying out this four-step process may seem like a near-impossible assignment. The feelings at the time when ego strikes can be very intense. Early on it may be wise to revisit the four steps after the dust settles and the intense pain subsides. Just know that it gets easier with each success. Your baby steps will gradually grow into giant steps. Before you know it, you will notice interpretation disappearing from the exact same situation that previously caused you pain. What remains is Spirit Consciousness, where you will begin to experience the happiness and peace of mind that you've always hoped to enjoy in your primary relationship.

* * *

One last thought on the subject of interpretation: Ego loves fatigue. When we grow tired our walls of defense against ego pain become porous. Ego can find its way into your feeling state more easily and before you know it ego consciousness has taken over the helm of your emotional ship. In a state of tiredness, it is much more difficult—especially when you are first learning to recognize the presence of ego in your life—to observe it and let it go. You feel easily flooded by ego when you're tired and the pain seems overwhelming.

To handle these difficult feelings from a Spiritual perspective, there are three things you can do. First, take every measure possible to stay rested. Nothing is more effective for holding ego at bay than getting the proper amount of sleep. This is a real issue in our lives today for several reasons. The level of stress that most people live with every day makes it more difficult to clear our minds to fall asleep. We tend to awaken in the middle of the night with so many things to think about that our minds begin racing. Also television sets, computers, and other electronic devices keep us up past the point that our bodies tell us that it is time to sleep.

Second, ego loves to bring up bothersome issues when you're the most tired. Try not to let this happen. Notice that this is ego trying to wedge its way in. Bring these issues up when you feel more rested. This will prevent ego flooding, which is always filled with excruciating pain. In this same vein, one man reported that he refuses to make a decision of any weight after 6:00 p.m. He knows if he does that ego can create blemishes in his thinking that inevitably lead him to pain.

Third, when you do get sucked into ego's vortex due to fatigue, be forgiving of yourself afterward when you look back and see what really took place. The mere recognition of the fact that ego was functioning at full strength and that you were temporarily under its spell is to be *in* Spirit at that moment. The more moments like this you have, the more your Spirit Consciousness will grow. As a result, ego will gradually recede and take with it the pain that has plagued you.

Chapter Twenty-Three

PRODUCTIVITY AND SPIRIT

Nearly everyone wants to be more productive in their lives. Whether it relates to work goals, family goals, or personal goals, productivity is about achieving the results you desire.

There are two ways to approach productivity: in a state of ego consciousness or in a state of Spirit Consciousness. Historically and still today, most productivity occurs in the context of ego consciousness. It is characterized by anxiety, stress, tight deadlines, pressure, strain, force, struggle, sweat, toil, and Herculean effort.

Let us use a business example to better understand this point. Suppose you need to complete a research assignment as soon as possible because a major project is being delayed pending the results of your study. Your manager is on your back about finalizing it. So you leave for work earlier than usual and skip breakfast in an attempt to complete the report. At the end of the workday, it still isn't finished. You stay late, which causes you to miss dinner. When you arrive home, your kids are fighting with each other because they're tired, waiting up after their bedtime to see you. Your husband is frustrated with the children and with you for working late. You're worn out but decide to spend some focused time with your family to help them relax. Things finally settle down and you fall into bed exhausted, but you still have trouble sleeping due to the stresses throughout the day. You decide to take a sleeping pill to knock yourself out. In the morning, you oversleep and arrive late to work. You miss the morning meeting where the report was to be distributed, and you end up rushing around to get a copy to everyone who would have normally received it in the meeting. You work hard the rest of the day, although you're very tired. After work you rush out to drive your kids to their various activities, and end up gulping down fast food for dinner on the way home.

So it goes when in the grip of ego consciousness. Each day differs only in the details. The constant is the stress you experience. Though you feel miserable, ego has accomplished its mission. By keeping you in a stress-filled life style every single day, ego lives on, and that—given its need for survival—is precisely its goal.

* * *

By contrast, productivity that comes from Spiritual Consciousness is joyful and peaceful. Ego-driven productivity is surrounded by pain, Spirit-related productivity is not. Productivity in Spirit Consciousness is characterized by understanding, harmony, mutual respect, collaboration, love, shared responsibility, peace of mind, happiness, and effortless accomplishment.

Let us revisit the research assignment, only this time let's approach it from a Spiritual perspective. Since your report is necessary to keep the project moving forward, and because you know it will be difficult to complete in a timely manner, you go to your manager and ask for help. You inquire if there are additional resources available that can be freed up for a short time to help you finish the research. If there are none, then you inform your manager that it is impossible to complete the report by yourself in the time remaining, and ask what he suggests can be done. If you must go into work early or stay late, you would discuss this with your husband and reach an understanding about the details for meals, children's bedtimes, and any other possible contingencies. You would make sure that you take care of your own needs for healthy nourishment and rest. You would arrange to get help to shuttle your children to and from their various activities, perhaps asking your husband if he can work out a plan to take care of the matter for you.

Note that it would be a mistake to conclude that if you do all these things, you will necessarily be operating from a state of Spirit Consciousness. This may not be the case at all. It is entirely possible to go through the same motions based on thinking these are the things you *should* do. If so, there will still be a high degree of stress, which means ego is involved.

Here is a more accurate statement: *If* you operate from Spirit, then these are the things that you *will* do. The reason is that when you're already in Spiritual Consciousness, you will choose behaviors that are consistent with the peacefulness and joy that are intrinsic to this state. Ego and "should" are twin sisters. If you operate from a mindset of what you should do, ego is in charge and you're functioning in a state of anxiety, pressure, and stress. If you proceed in a Spiritual mindset, there are no shoulds. You are free to choose, and in that freedom, you will choose the peaceful path.

* * *

For many people it is counterintuitive that Spirit Consciousness actually leads to more productivity than ego consciousness. Just because Spirit Consciousness is more effortless, that does not mean that it accomplishes less. The notion that hard-driving, pressure-filled work leads to more productivity is one that has been planted firmly by ego, where the rules are that you must suffer in order to accomplish anything. It is grounded in the concept of competition—doing things in the fastest possible way, getting ahead, beating the other guy, and excelling over others.

In Spirit Consciousness productivity is more the result of *coopetition* rather than of *competition*. It fosters cooperation, coordinated effort, collaboration, and shared responsibility. It is a matter of everyone willingly pulling on the same rope in the same direction. This principle applies to every situation where productivity is the goal; no matter if it relates to raising children, clearing a field of trees and stones, working on a project in business, teaching a group of students, leading and managing employees, coaching an athletic team, running your own business, constructing houses, or building highways. Spirit Consciousness will lead you to more productivity than ego consciousness, every time.

If you're thinking at this point that hard work is indeed sometimes necessary to be productive, certainly that is true. But hard work per se is not the issue. The issue is whether or not the hard work is a matter of choice or pressure. Hard work that is freely chosen is an act of Spirit. Hard work that is driven by pressure, regardless of whether it is self-imposed or from an external source, is an act of ego. The exception would be if one chooses pressure-filled work, but even then, the fact that one has chosen it mitigates the stress, which still renders it an act of Spirit.

If you want to raise your level of productivity, you can *try* to be more collaborative, *try* to be more cooperative, and *try* to work with others in a mindset of mutual respect and shared responsibility. But all this *trying* can be a long and hard road, and you may or may not eventually get there. The challenge is that if you attempt to change your behavior while still functioning in ego consciousness, you are likely to backslide because ego will, more than likely, find ways to sabotage your efforts.

The most efficient and painless way to become more productive is to move beyond the ego into the world of Spirit. Once there, all the things required to be productive may come to you naturally and effortlessly without you forcing anything. It is not the nature of Spirit to force. It is the nature of Spirit to *join forces* to achieve the results you desire.

Part VI

Spirit Has a
Language
of Its Own

Chapter Twenty-Four

LANGUAGE BEYOND THE EGO

Clearly, ego has a language of its own. It has been with us all of our lives. It is deeply built into the fabric of how we think and speak. Ego language is a confluence of concepts and words that represent the discontentment, disappointment, and suffering inherent in ego consciousness. It includes such notions as:

Judgment	Criticism
Egocentricity	Selfishness
Piety	Self-righteousness
Indignation	Rebuke
Achievement	Wealth
Attachment	Anger
Loneliness	Frustration
Apathy	Aggression
Pride	Antagonism
Hopelessness	Evil
Blame	Humiliation
Reactivity	Self-condemnation
One-upmanship	Superiority
Accumulation	Fear
Indifference	Guilt

Disgrace   Regret
Shame   Worry

This is a mere sampling of ego concepts; there are countless others. Thinking and speaking within the framework of ego consciousness is so habitual and unconscious that it would be difficult to identify them all. Ego language is so common in our daily communications that it is accepted as the normal means of discourse.

* * *

Ego language is not the original cause of our suffering. The real cause is the belief that we are separate and disconnected entities in the world. Ego language is simply the way we've learned to express the pervasive unhappiness and unrest that results from this belief.

Nevertheless, ego language plays a large role in sustaining ego consciousness and perpetuating human suffering; it becomes the conceptual and moral infrastructure for the institutions that support and sustain ego's ways. Family, friends, religion, politics, education, medicine, law, science, business, social services, athletics, advertising, and so on are all laced with ego language. Nothing escapes its influence. As such, it contributes heavily toward keeping dissatisfaction and suffering at the forefront of human experience.

* * *

To facilitate and support your journey beyond the ego, it will be of great help to learn the language of Spirit. As you move beyond the ego, its language will gradually subside, thus leaving a vacuum. It is important that you fill this vacuum with the language of Spirit. Otherwise, ego language, in its attempts to survive, will rush back in to fill the void.

Know too that this is not a case of your new Spirit language trying to shove the ego language out. Remember, don't push—it prolongs the process. Rather, the new language merely fills the hole left by the shrinking ego. In effect, what this does is leave fewer and fewer places for ego to grab hold. As you move to substitute the new language for the old, be attentive to the concepts that reflect the language of Spirit. Among them are:

Peace	Joy
Happiness	Harmony
Acceptance	Forgiveness
Meaning	Transformation
Serenity	Affirmation
Charity	Benevolence
Support	Empathy
Collaboration	Compassion
Patience	Reverence
Purpose	Silence
Cooperation	Inspiration
Love	Hope
Understanding	Trust
Helpfulness	Satisfaction
Respect	Care
Optimism	Altruism
Generosity	Sympathy

Try to be patient with yourself as you make the transition. The language of Spirit will take time to master because language is one of ego's greatest strongholds. To become aware of ego—to watch it and study it—is also to become aware of ego's language and to watch and study it as well.

When you hear yourself thinking or saying something that gives even the slightest hint that ego is involved, one of the things you can do to help transition from ego language to Spirit language is to reframe your thought or statement in the words of Spirit. The next two chapters provide a number of examples and tools to help you accomplish this goal.

Chapter Twenty-Five

SPIRIT IS FREE FROM JUDGMENT

Judgmental words sustain and perpetuate ego consciousness, regardless of whether they are thought or spoken. "Judgment" in this context means the act of passing moral or personal judgment on oneself or others.

Nearly everyone makes judgments, some more than others. Even people who are intent on not making judgments typically do so more often than they realize. Judgmental words in our language are commonplace to the extent that we generally aren't aware that we use them. Ego loves this unconsciousness. Unawareness creates a medium in which ego can multiply and survive through the suffering that judgment causes us. Byron Katie,[1] in her national bestseller *Loving What Is,* speaks to the issue of suffering and judgment:

> The only time we suffer is when we believe a thought that argues with what is....And yet, if you pay attention, you'll notice that you think [judgmental] thoughts like this dozens of times a day. "People should be kinder." "Children should be well-behaved." "My neighbors should take better care of their lawn." "The line at the grocery store

should move faster." "My husband (or wife) should agree with me." "I should be thinner (or prettier or more successful)." These thoughts are ways of wanting reality to be different than it is. If you think that this sounds depressing, you're right. All the stress that we feel is caused by arguing with what is.

In addition to the suffering that judgment making causes, it is also a clear act of one-upmanship, whether you're passing judgment on one or more persons, or even when you judge yourself. When you judge another, the message conveyed is that *"I know better than you,"* or *"I am better than you"*; ego thrives on both of these. When you judge yourself, the insinuation is that "I in-the-present" know better than "I in-the-past," which makes me one up in the *now*. This is another example of how subtle ego can be.

* * *

Beyond question, the most commonly used words that express judgments are:

should/shouldn't
ought/ought not
good/bad
right/wrong

Listen to yourself and to others talk. Observe the thoughts that go through your mind about your own behavior and the behavior of others. Pay attention to the language of others when you talk with them. Listen to the news or watch a movie. You will hear these judgmental words popping up in nearly every conversation, usually multiple times.

"I'm going to be late for work; I *should* have taken a different route."

"You made a *bad* decision when you traded in your old car."

"You *ought not* to watch TV until you get your homework done."

"You did the *right* thing by supporting your wife's decision to go back to college."

"It's *wrong* to talk about other people that way."

"The temperatures aren't where they *ought* to be at this time of year."

"That was a *good* meal we had at the restaurant tonight."

"Relax; you *shouldn't* take everything so seriously."

You may be asking yourself, "What's *wrong* with using these common words? Most people use them all the time, including me. What's the problem?"

First of all, there is nothing right or wrong, good or bad about using words that convey judgment. Either you do or you don't. That's the way it is. The point is that for those of you who aspire to travel beyond the ego, your transition will be more expeditious if you pay attention to the frequency with which these common judgmental words are used.

Granted, many such words have multiple meanings. "Good," for example, can mean *bountiful*, as in "good" land; *handsome*, as in "good" looking; *amusing*, as in "good" joke; *well-founded*, as in "good" reasons; and so on. Yet each is a judgment in that value is placed on one thing over another. In ego's view, a good joke is superior to a bad joke; good looking is superior to bad looking; and a good movie is superior to a bad one. But we must keep in mind that preference and judgment are two different things. You can prefer something without judging it. For example, preferring one joke to another does not convey judgment; suggesting that one joke is superior to another does. *Anytime superiority or inferiority is at issue, judgment is present and hence, so is ego.*

* * *

The bigger point is, if you use words that express judgment in situations where judgment isn't at issue—for example, "You are *right* that $1 + 1 = 2$"—you risk missing how ego utilizes this same word in situations that *are* clearly judgmental. Familiarity may indeed breed contempt. But when it comes to ego, familiarity through frequent use of potentially judgmental words breeds generalized application of those words. To ego it is a short jump from "You are *right* that $1 + 1 = 2$"—a statement of fact—to "You were *right* to leave your spouse," which is a moral judgment. In other words, *the more freely we use judgmental terms in factual applications, the less aware we become when ego uses these terms to pass judgment in moral situations.*

If one could be totally aware one hundred percent of the time, one would be able to discern the difference between "innocent" uses of a judgmental expression versus more "malicious" ones. Since few people are perfectly aware one hundred percent of the time, ego will disappear more easily if you attempt to eliminate these words from your vocabulary altogether. The way to do this is to replace potentially judgmental words with factual words that will still accurately—and in fact, more precisely—convey your intended meaning. For example, it could be said just as precisely, "You are *accurate* (or *correct*) that $1 + 1 = 2$," rather than *right*; one can be referred to as *handsome* instead of *good* looking; and land can be called *fruitful* or *productive* rather than *good* land.

In other words, language can be very lazy. This is particularly true of the judgmental words should/shouldn't, ought/ought not, right/wrong, and good/bad. They tend to become multipurpose terms that ego applies to a variety of situations in order to make its insidious presence more and more transparent.

With only a little effort this tendency can be reversed. If you've ever listened to someone speak in purely descriptive terms as opposed to judgmental ones, you will know how delightfully refreshing judgment-free language can be. For example, instead of referring to your new employment as a *good* job, you might describe it as meaningful, rewarding, challenging, or high-income; perhaps one with convenient work hours, friendly associates, or built-in job security. Rather than call a young lad a *bad* boy, one could just as easily describe him as misbehaved, ill-mannered, disobedient, undisciplined, or uncontrolled, depending on the context.

* * *

To become more familiar with alternative ways of expressing yourself using descriptive rather than judgmental language, consider the following examples.

Ego: "I *shouldn't* have eaten so much."

Spirit: "I feel bloated when I eat so much."
"If I hadn't eaten so much, I wouldn't feel so bloated."
"I wish I hadn't eaten so much."
"I ate too much."
"I'm stuffed!"

Ego: "You are *wrong*, son, for not going to college."

Spirit: "You might be making a mistake by not going to college."
"What do you think your challenges might be if you don't attend college?"

"I've wished that I had gone to college, and it's something I've hoped you would do."

"I disagree with your decision to not attend college, but I respect it."

Ego: "I was *right* when I told my supervisor that he didn't know what he was talking about."

Spirit: "I disagreed with my supervisor on what needed to be done, but in the end he decided to do it another way."

"I saw the situation quite differently than my supervisor did, but I respected that it was his responsibility to make the final decision."

"My experience told me what needed to be done, but he didn't see it the same way."

Ego: "I *ought* to get more exercise."

Spirit: "I need to get more exercise."

"I'd like to get more exercise."

"If I get more exercise, I'll be healthier and feel much better."

"I'd be wise to get more exercise."

* * *

Thus far, the emphasis placed on judgmental thinking has been limited to should/shouldn't, ought/ought not, good/bad, and right/wrong because these are the most common judgmental concepts in ego language. But there are countless other terms that express judgment. In an ego-centered world judgment runs rampant. It is only to be expected that language will reflect this judgment. This is why language in general is swollen with a multiplicity of concepts where the intent to be one up is already built into their meaning.

Caution is required here because only a small percentage of judgment is contained in the actual word(s): approximately seven to ten percent. The remainder lies in the intent, tone, and body language of the person making the judgment.

This principle is difficult to demonstrate on paper, but let's try. Imagine someone describing a man to another person in a gentle and professional way, "He is dirty," with the intent of being as factual as possible about his lack of cleanliness. Compare this with another person in the same situation saying in a raised voice and with a disgusted look, "*He* is *dirty!*" with the intent of looking down on him.

That said, what follows is a partial list of potentially judgmental terms, along with alternatives for how to describe someone with less risk of judging them. If you take exception to anything on the list, try to keep two things in mind. First, tone, body language, and intent play the largest role in whether or not a word is judgmental, and as mentioned, this cannot be given full justice on paper.

Second, the focus here is entirely about judging people, not things. So think of each word as an adjective that might be used to describe an individual. Adjectives are used as examples because this is how most judgments are made—he is an *obnoxious* person, she is *overbearing,* or they are a *strange* family. There are many other terms that express judgment that are not adjectives: *jerk, psycho, cheapskate,* and *scoundrel,* to name a few. Once you get a feel for concepts that tend to convey judgment, you will begin to recognize that all four main parts of speech—nouns, verbs, adjectives, and adverbs—can, and often do, imply judgment.

* * *

Judgmental Adjectives	Less Judgmental Alternatives
abrasive	irritating
abusive	hurtful
addicted	dependent on
aloof	distant or uninvolved
annoying	bothersome
arrogant	swollen self-concept
awful	extreme
bad	unacceptable
belligerent	argumentative
boastful	exaggerating of self
boring	tiring
callous	unfeeling
careless	indifferent to detail or risk
cheap	frugal
clumsy	lacks coordination
combative	quick to fight or argue
contentious	willing to quarrel
controlling	influences others for personal gain
cowardly	timid
cranky	easily angered
crazy	exhibits unusual behavior
creepy	unpleasant or scary to be around
cruel	disposed to inflict pain
cynical	disbelieving of one's sincerity
dangerous	capable of inflicting harm
deceitful	misleading
defective	imperfect
defiant	challenges authority

demonic	ill-disposed
deranged	incoherent
disgusting	prone to offensive behavior
disturbed	not OK mentally
domineering	demanding to have control over others
dull	slow
dumb	mentally challenged
erratic	behaves inconsistently
evasive	avoiding
evil	extremely unacceptable
fanatical	intensely and uncritically devoted
fat	plump
filthy	excessively dirty
finicky	exacting in taste or standards
flippant	lacking respect
foolish	simple
fretful	worried
gluttonous	voracious
greedy	eager to acquire
grouchy	peevish
gruesome	frightful
grumpy	complaining
gullible	easily cheated
helpless	defenseless
horrible	extremely unpleasant
hysterical	filled with excessive fear or laughter
idiotic	lacking in common sense
ignorant	unaware or uninformed

immature	exhibits behavior not becoming of one's age
incompetent	inadequate knowledge for a particular purpose
insensitive	uncaring
lazy	not energetic
loathsome	offensive
loony	exhibits unusual behavior
manipulative	controlling for one's own advantage
materialistic	preoccupied with material things
mean	hurtful
miserly	scant in giving or spending
mysterious	possessing an inexplicable characteristic
nagging	complaining
naïve	unaware
narcissistic	loves oneself excessively
nasty	spiteful
naughty	misbehaved
nuts	exhibits unusual behavior
obnoxious	offensive
outrageous	unrestrained
pathetic	sad
possessive	dominating desire to own things
promiscuous	not restricted to one person
psychotic	exhibits unusual behavior
pudgy	plump
queer	gay
relentless	unwilling to soften or yield

repulsive	offensive
ruthless	without mercy
sassy	impudent
schizoid	exhibits unusual behavior
secretive	withholding
selfish	putting oneself ahead of others
shameful	questionable
sinister	with mal-intent
skinny	thin
slovenly	untidy
sluttish	loose
snobbish	offensively superior
stingy	scant in giving or spending
strange	unusual
stupid	unthinking
tacky	lacks style or taste
terrible	extreme
thoughtless	careless or unconcerned
tight	scant in giving or spending
timid	shy
ugly	unpleasant to the senses
uptight	tense or nervous
vengeful	seeking to avenge
volatile	prone to explosiveness
vulgar	indecent
weak	frail or fragile
whiny	complaining
wicked	likely to cause harm
worthless	lacking value
wretched	distressed

* * *

How important is it, really, to avoid using judgmental language? What does it matter if you say it one way instead of another?

It only matters in one sense. If you are earnest about going beyond the ego, you will find that purging your vocabulary of common judgmental terms can be helpful as a means to expedite your journey from ego to Spirit. It is similar to surgically removing cancer: you would want to remove every possible trace of it if the goal is to minimize the odds that it may return.

That being said, here are three additional tips to help you make the transition:

- Eliminating from your vocabulary words that judge doesn't happen overnight. First you will need to identify them. Once you accomplish that, you can begin substituting descriptive words for the judgmental ones. Many people find this to be a fun, although at times, challenging exercise.

- Try to refrain from judging others when you hear them use the same words that you're attempting to remove from your own vocabulary. This would be a clever maneuver of the ego, would it not—to pass judgment on other people's use of judgmental words at the same time that you're working to eliminate your own?

- Even when you become proficient at refraining from the use of judgmental words, you may still notice that occasionally they sneak in here and there. This is to be expected since you've learned—and spoken—ego's language from the time you were born. The very fact that you are able to spot judgmental words even after you express them tells you that Spirit is—and will continue to be—your trusted guide on the other side of the ego.

Chapter Twenty-Six

FINE-TUNING THE LANGUAGE OF SPIRIT

There are two cardinal rules for making the transition from ego language to Spirit language. The first is that *your opportunity to transition is always now.* It is present here, in this moment. The instant you discover yourself using ego language, make your best attempt to restate whatever you said or thought by using the language of Spirit.

The second rule is that *it is never too late* to deepen your Spiritual journey even if you feel that your ego language has offended another person. You may discover that you've said something that was hurtful to a friend, colleague, or loved one. As soon as you become aware that this was your ego doing the talking, go to that person, apologize, and then state what you meant to say in the language of Spirit. Doing so is a powerful Spiritual experience. It will help heal the offended person, it will feel loving and joyful to you, and it will be one more step—a giant step, actually—toward letting your ego lapse into a permanent and peaceful slumber.

These same principles also apply to language you use to talk to yourself. Suppose you catch yourself thinking thoughts that are self-critical: "Why did you say that, stupid?" "I never should have addressed the problem in that way!" "What an idiot!" Just remember, *your opportunity to transition is always now* and *it is never too late*. Self-criticism is always ego speaking. As soon as you notice it happening, replace your words with Spirit language: "I can see how I could have said that differently." "I didn't mean to offend anyone." "I want to make an apology and then say what I meant in a different way."

Making this shift from ego language to Spiritual language amounts to telling yourself the truth. It is not the truth that you are stupid, that you shouldn't have said what you did, or that you're an idiot. Each of these statements is a judgment and judgments are made of ego stuff. The truth is, whatever you said didn't sit well with you, there are other ways to approach the problem, and an apology may be in order. Spirit is loving and understanding. By using its language, you will feel happier, be more at peace, and find renewed energy to continue on with life.

* * *

In the beginning, transitioning from the language of ego to the language of Spirit requires a concentrated effort on your part. However, it becomes second nature rather quickly if you give it a fair try.

Becoming more familiar with how this transition can occur may help you in your journey. To that end, the remainder of the chapter is given to comparing and contrasting the differences between how ego and Spirit might respond to various real-life situations. If the examples presented are not ones you've ever found yourself in, try not to let this get in the way of your learning. The idea is to look at how ego inserts itself into our daily thoughts and language and examine how you might replace ego's language with the language of Spirit. The more you can do so, the more your ego loses its influence in your life.

* * *

Situation: You pull up to the gas pump and it has an "out of order" sign on it.

Ego Thinking: "Wouldn't you know it; just my luck when I'm in a hurry!"

Spirit Thinking: "Apparently this pump isn't working. I'll need to find another one."

* * *

Situation: Your spouse asks you to do something for her and you're in the middle of another project.

Ego Speaking: "What I'm doing never matters to you, does it! You're always bugging me about something. Get off my case and leave me alone!"

Spirit Speaking: "I'm busy right now, dear. Does it need to be done immediately or can it wait until I finish what I'm working on?"

* * *

Situation: You are cleaning the house after having asked your daughter to help out. She had other plans and no one else is home.

Ego Thinking: "Why am I the one who always does the cleaning? This just isn't fair. Someone else ought to get off their derriere and help out once in a while.

I'm sick and tired of being taken for granted!"

Spirit Thinking: "I'd like more help with the housework. I think we'll sit down as a family and devise a plan where everyone does their fair share."

* * *

Situation: You are approaching the shopping mall looking for a place to park. You spot an opening and just as you are about to pull in the driver of another car zooms into the space you intended to use.

Ego Thinking: "You jerk! That was my parking spot and you stole it. I'd like to punch your headlights out. Some people don't have any manners, you selfish moron!"

Spirit Thinking: "Interesting behavior. He must have needed that parking place more than I did. I'm sure I can find another spot to park."

* * *

Situation: You are standing in line at the checkout register and someone cuts in front of you.

Ego Speaking: "Excuse me but I was here first. Go to the back of the line where you belong."

Spirit Speaking: "Hello, sir. Did you mean to cut in front of me?"

* * *

Situation: You see an advertisement in the paper for an automobile that you might be interested in buying. You place a call and learn that it has already been sold. You say to the person on the other end of the phone:

Ego Speaking: "Wouldn't you know it; I never have any luck. I'm always a day late and a dollar short!"

Spirit Speaking: "I would like to have seen the car, but I'm happy you were able to sell it."

* * *

Situation: Your teenager's curfew is 11:00 p.m. and he arrives home at 12:20 a.m. You've waited up for him to make sure he's OK.

Ego Speaking: "Where in God's creation have you been? Doesn't your curfew mean anything to you? I knew I shouldn't have trusted you. You never do anything you're expected to do."

Spirit Speaking: "It's past your curfew and I've been worried about you. Are you OK? Did something come up? What does it mean that you broke your curfew? What do you think needs to happen

173

now?" (with pauses between each question to hear your son's answers)

* * *

Situation: Your two-year-old daughter keeps throwing her food on the floor during dinner.

Ego Speaking: "Stop! That's naughty. You're a bad little girl."

Spirit Speaking: "Mommy doesn't like it when you throw your food on the floor. I'd like you to stop. When you do I'll give you more food, but not before."

* * *

Situation: One of your colleagues at work has a complaint about you and goes to your manager instead of coming directly to you. The manager calls you into her office to report what happened.

Ego Speaking: "That makes me so mad! She's always trying to get other people in trouble by tattling on them. I knew it was just a matter of time before she did that to me."

Spirit Speaking: "The fact that she didn't come to me makes me wonder if I'm difficult to approach. Do you have any ideas how I could make it easier for her to bring her concerns directly to me, so we can work them out together?"

* * *

Situation: Recently, your mother-in-law moved into your home because she's dying of cancer. You're working hard to get her house in order so it can be put on the market. Your wife's sister approaches you and criticizes how you've boxed up her mother's belongings.

Ego Speaking: "You can't seem to find time to help with your mother's care but you seem to have plenty of time to criticize me. Why don't you pitch in and help instead of finding fault with everything I do!"

Spirit Speaking: "I know it must be hard to watch your mother die yet not be able to do anything about it. How about giving me a hand and we'll talk about it together."

* * *

Situation: Your teenage daughter comes to the breakfast table dressed for school in clothes you don't approve of.

Ego Speaking: "Don't think for a minute you're going to wear that blouse to school! That will give you a reputation that will be impossible to live down. Go change into something more respectable!"

Spirit Speaking: "Honey, I have some concerns about the blouse you're wearing this morning. I'd like to talk about it with you, but I know we don't have time right now. Would you mind wearing something different for today, and then we can talk about it this evening. It would mean a lot to me if you would do this."

* * *

Situation: You've overheard some gossip about your neighbor, Sylvia, and you're eager to tell someone about it. You call a friend.

Ego Speaking: "Guess what I heard. Sylvia's son who's away at college was arrested yesterday for selling drugs! Can you believe it?"

Spirit Speaking: Option 1: Don't mention it to your friend. Option 2: "My neighbor, Sylvia, is dealing with some challenges concerning her son. I'm not sure exactly what's going on but I think I'll ask her if she'd like to talk or if I can be of any help."

* * *

Situation: You plan to attend an outdoor concert and you aren't sure whether to take your umbrella with you. You tune into the local weather report and learn that it's predicted to be sunny and warm for the next forty-eight hours. You decide to leave your umbrella at home. One hour into the concert there is a cloudburst and you get drenched.

Ego Thinking: "Those meteorologists don't know what they're talking about! They're wrong half of the time. Why do I bother to listen to them?"

Spirit Thinking: "I can only imagine how embarrassed the meteorologist I listened to must be. It's got to be difficult to predict the weather. I think in the future I'll plan to take my umbrella along regardless what the weather report is."

* * *

Are you thinking that you'd never be able to respond like this, or maybe that you wouldn't want to? The point is not that you *should* think or speak in any prescribed way. These examples are intended only to demonstrate the difference between an egoic response to a difficult situation as compared with a Spiritual one.

Ego wants to react, accuse, be right, dominate, gossip, defend, demand, feel victimized, and so on. Each of these has the potential to cause you or someone you're interacting with to be upset. When either party is upset, ego is contented because it knows it will live on.

Spirit acts with love and understanding. It wants to solve problems not make them. It wants you to be joyful and at peace. In any problematic situation that might arise, if you ask yourself the question, "How can I express love and understanding in this situation?" then you have both feet planted firmly in the world of

Spirit. You are happy and sleep well at night. You have a smile on your face because you *love life*. And you don't fear death because you know in your soul that you are living the essence of what it means to be fully human, both in this life and beyond.

Part VII

Conclusion

Chapter Twenty-Seven

THE CHOICE IS YOURS

In the bigger scheme of things, we humans are much like the "Whos" in the children's book by Dr. Seuss, *Horton Hears a Who*. We are little creatures in the cosmos living on a tiny speck of dust, which in the book was called "Whoville." We call ours planet Earth. Frasier Cain,[1] publisher of *Universe Today*, states it more succinctly: "Our Earth feels like all there is, but we know that it's just a tiny planet in a vast Solar System. And our Solar System is just one member of a vast Milky Way galaxy with 200 to 400 billion stars. ..[and] there are 100 to 200 billion galaxies in the Universe, each of which has hundreds of billions of stars."

If that isn't sufficient to make you feel insignificant, consider this fact. The earth is approximately five billion years old. By comparison, records of human history date back only ten thousand years. If we condense the age of earth into one calendar year beginning at midnight on January 1 and the present moment is a fraction before midnight one year hence, then human beings appeared on the scene around 11:58:30 p.m. on December 31, the emperor Nero ruled Rome at 11:59:42 p.m., and the United States declared its independence as a nation at 11:59:56 p.m.

* * *

However tiny or insignificant we may feel in the unfathomable expansiveness of the universe, intuitively we know we count for something. We are here, after all, in spite of the fact that no one knows for certain how or why. Being here, we search for the definition of who we are as beings and where we fit in the bigger picture.

At the most basic level, there are only two possibilities. Either we are inextricably connected to this vast cosmos or we are separate from it. Our earliest experiences in life teach us that we are the latter of the two—isolated, separated, and disconnected beings. Society—which is an accumulation of fellow beings who also feel isolated and disconnected—supports, sustains, and perpetuates this belief for the rest of our lives. It becomes the defining factor for how we experience our"selves"—our sense of "I"ness—which we call ego.

Given this mistaken definition of who we are as beings, we are left to fend for ourselves in a large, alien world. Since in that context we feel small, insignificant, unimportant, and irrelevant, we must behave in ways that bolster our defenses. We accomplish this by compensating, which is acting out behaviors that are the exact opposite of what we really feel inside. This means we must act powerful, self-important, big, significant, right, authoritative, and judgmental—in a word, one up on all others. This is the way our sense of "self"—our ego—works to ensure its own survival. The result is a universal superiority complex that is the fountainhead of human suffering.

This suffering manifests itself in three dimensions. First, the thirst for superiority is extreme for many people. The more superior they feel—whether through fame, fortune, influence, power, or wealth—the more one up they try to become. Over time, their dependence on superiority becomes so out of control that they eventually crash and burn. They fall from their pedestal in one way or another: legal infractions, moral violations, emotional or physical collapse, and other similar outcomes.

Second, acting superior is rarely received well by others and therefore often ends in suffering for the perpetrator. People who feel offended by those who act superior tend to criticize, shun, resist, and sometimes retaliate against them. For instance, individuals who try to control the behavior of others often strain even their closest relationships to the breaking point, causing the controlling individual to feel misunderstood, hurt, and lonely.

Third, acting superior toward others is a source of widespread suffering for those on the receiving end. One spouse might act superior to the other in ways that cause fierce arguments, relentless criticisms, or broken relationships. Parents say and do—or don't say and do—things that can be excruciatingly painful to their children, even though it is usually unintentional and often very subtle. Controlling behaviors, manipulative interactions, and endless judgments by people in positions of authority and power—e.g., parents and employers—can cause those who are directly affected to be frightened, hurt, depressed, ashamed, and angry. These types of feelings lead to an endless stream of suffering: chronic physical and emotional illnesses, drug addiction, alcoholism, revenge, shootings, suicides, and repressed pain that resurfaces in adulthood, especially in close relationships.

These same acts of superiority are a source of environmental pollution, international conflict, economic instability, weapons of mass destruction, terrorism, global unrest, and the never-ending threat of self-destruction as a species.

This constant march toward superiority is the nature of ego. It is grounded in the misidentification of who we are as beings. To protect and preserve this mistaken identity and thus ensure its survival, ego causes us to behave in ways that contradict who we really are as beings, producing both personal and large-scale suffering. In essence, the gap between who we think we are and who we are in actuality produces an effect in us akin to coarse sandpaper being rubbed against our souls.

Whether viewed in the microcosm of the individual or the macrocosm of society at large, this state of being—ego consciousness—is hell. It is a state of mind, an inner space of misery and unrest, dissatisfaction and suffering. We know this because we've experienced it all too often. And experience being the teacher of all things, we know that hell exists in the *now*, here on earth.

* * *

The other choice in our search to define who we are as beings is to view ourselves as fundamentally connected to the cosmos— an inseparable part of everything. Recent findings in quantum physics confirm this—that everything is made of the same conscious "stuff," everything is sustained by the same animating force (Spirit), and we are all one.

When viewed from this perspective, there is no need to act powerful, important, superior, right, hurried, authoritative, entitled, and judgmental. Instead, it positions our existence as an opportunity to act lovingly toward everyone and everything, to show humility in all things, to understand, empathize, show compassion, and make charity toward others our primary focus. These are qualities of Spirit. Freely expressing them soothes our souls. It resonates with who we are as beings. It fills us with joy and a sense of inner peace.

This state of being is called heaven. Traditionally, heaven is thought to be a place for reward after death. But like hell, heaven is a state of mind: an inner space of contentment, serene happiness, peace of mind, love, and well-being. We've all had opportunities to touch it—the birth of a child, the love of a parent, sitting by the shore at sunset, observing a beautiful flower, standing at a height where you can see clearly in all directions, holding the hand of a loved one as he or she dies in peace. These are sacred things. There is no signage to tell us so; we just know it to be true. We know it because it resonates within our souls. It is Spirit reminding us of who we are. And to this extent we know that heaven, like hell, exists in the *now*, here on earth.

* * *

To enjoy heaven on earth rather than suffer its hell is determined by which is in charge: Spirit or ego. You have a choice about this. If you don't choose, you are automatically in the grip of ego.

To be free to choose Spirit Consciousness over ego consciousness is to understand the differences between the two. They are not in conflict with one another; they simply exist in different dimensions. Ego is manufactured by the human psyche; Spirit is universal intelligence. Ego is our mistaken definition of who we are: separate and disconnected beings alone in an alien world. Spirit is the divine force that sets the world in motion and then sustains it.

A key point to understand here is that *ego cannot discover, acknowledge, or observe Spirit.* To do so would expose ego, thus causing its own demise. To the contrary, *Spirit is fully capable of discovering, acknowledging, and observing ego.* Spirit isn't threatened by ego because it isn't concerned about surviving. Spirit knows it is eternal. It is here now, in the moment, forever.

Spirit and ego are both accessed by looking inside, since that is where they reside. Your job is to find ego. Look for it, watch it, listen to its voice trying to stir up trouble, act superior, or cause pain and suffering to you or another person. When you find it, at that moment you are *in* Spirit. *This is your first giant step into the Spiritual world.*

When Spirit watches ego, something magical happens. Ego suddenly quiets down. Spirit is sunshine; ego is darkness. Put the two together and sunshine will prevail. This is the way Spirit puts ego to rest. Not by crushing it or trying to destroy it, but by merely noticing it. Ego cannot survive when it is being watched, just as darkness cannot survive in the presence of light.

You have this choice: ego or Spirit. It is not a group decision; it is a very personal decision that everyone must make. Again, to not choose is choosing to let ego stay in control. To choose to grow in Spiritual Consciousness is your pathway to enlightenment, your salvation from mental and emotional pain and suffering. Since we live in the flesh, we will still experience physical pain at times. Yet living in the Spirit brings a qualitative difference to physical pain. It is accepted more than fought, to some degree distance is put between the two, and physical pain ceases to be as problematic.

* * *

A question often comes up at this point: If heaven and hell are here and now, what happens after our physical bodies die? For ego, death is the ultimate phantom that lurks somewhere in the mystery of the future. For Spirit, it has meaning only as an abstraction in thought, which exists in the form of an anticipation of the future. In other words, death is real only insofar as we dread or fear it *now*, and hence bring it into present experience.

At the very instant when physical death arrives, as it will for all, it cannot be more or less than a new *now* experience. To give it our full attention—as much as possible at that moment—can only mean that we are alive in Spirit, which is to be alive in the fullest sense of the word. It is unique to humankind to be anxious about impending death. Living in such fear is to be dead to the reality of the moment, which—since *now* is all there is—is very much akin to being dead altogether.

This, of course, is not to say that one wouldn't take every precaution to protect against physical death. It would be unthinking to leave poisons under the kitchen sink with small children in the home or to drive a hundred miles per hour down the middle of the freeway on the way to work. But there is certainly a distinction between wanting to live, which is Spirit, and fearing to die, which is ego.

We are Spiritual beings having an ego experience. At the moment of death, our Spirit leaves our body—its temporary human home. But it lives on, now and forever. It is void of ego and lives in pure love and harmony, in peace and joy. This is Spirit's essence.

In our society, we tend to be distanced from death. We hide it in hospitals and nursing homes. Anyone who has journeyed to physical death with a loved one knows firsthand what a sacred experience this is. To see Spirit enter the body at birth is awe inspiring; to see it leave the body at physical death is sublime. And to know that your loved one is free from ego for eternity is peaceful and quieting. Of course there will be a period of sadness. All species grieve the loss of those whom they love. Yet through it all, you will know that your loved one's Spirit is alive and well and all pain and suffering are finally over.

* * *

If you feel moved to do so, sometime soon venture out on a clear night to a quiet spot, preferably away from city lights. Breathe deeply and look up at the vastness of the universe—the moon, the stars twinkling in the sky—and be reminded that you are looking at you. Be aware, as Wayne Dyer[2] writes, "… [that] Spirit is present in its entirety everywhere, which includes you. You can never ever be separated from it. You'll learn to laugh at the absurd idea that you could ever be separate from the universal mind. It's your Source. You are it."

Close your eyes and think of your loved ones, and know that they are you and you are them. Feel the presence of Spirit and know that it is the essence of all things. Know that because you are Spirit, you are one with all things. Feel the truth that we are all made of the same raw material, which is Pure Consciousness. If a loved one has accompanied you, look into his or her eyes and know that you are looking into your own soul. Take a moment and pet your dog, if you took it along. It is you and you are it. Feel the joy that surges through your body, knowing that you are not alone in the universe; you are an inseparable part of it all. Think for a moment what the world would be like if everyone could feel the love in all things, including the love for each other; if they could know their egos well enough to rise above them and live in peace; and if they could feel the soulful happiness of simply being.

We can only hope that day may come. It *will* come if everyone does his or her part. Your part is to find your own ego and keep it under your watchful eye without judging it. To do so is to raise your consciousness to the level of Spirit. You may recall that David R. Hawkins,[3] M.D., Ph.D., said, "To become more conscious is the greatest gift anyone can give to the world." Discover your ego, observe it, embrace it, and appreciate it for how hard it has worked to get you to where you are now. Doing these things will keep it in check until it rests in peace in the loving arms of Spirit.

As you do this you will find that the joy, peace, and love that you've long sought have begun to fill your cup. It is not necessary to wait to receive these blessings until the next life. They are yours for the taking *now*.

In time, you will complete your journey into ego and beyond, which is your mission while in the flesh. Fear not what happens when the flesh is gone. Spirit is eternal and the happiness, joy, peace, and love that are grounded in Spirit are your birthrights and the only things that last forever.

Notes

Chapter One

1. Tolle, Eckhart, *A New Earth* (New York: Dutton, 2005) 18–19.

Chapter Three

1. Goswami, Amit, interview by Craig Hamilton, TWM Breakthrough Technology, http://homepage. ihug.co.nz/~sai/goswam1.htm.

2. Wilber, Ken, *Up From Eden* (Wheaton: Theosophical, 1981), http://www.woopidoo.com/business_ quotes/authors/ken-wilber/index.htm.

Chapter Four

1. Van Cleve, Ken, "Panpsychism Explained," Panpsychism and Pantheism, http://www.panpsychism.net/ html/panpsychism_explained.html.

2. Holt, Jim, "Mind of a Rock," *New York Times*, November 18, 2007, http://www.nytimes. com/2007/11/18/magazine/18wwln-lede-t.html.

3. de Quincey, Christian, "Nature Has a Mind of Its Own," Integral Visioning, http://integralvisioning. org/article.php?story=cdq-radical-nature.

Chapter Five

1. Allon, Charles, "Plants as Sensitive Agents," Borderland Sciences Research Foundation, http://www. borderlands.com/newstuff/research/plantsas.htm.

2. Barber, Susan, "The Secret Life of Plants and Diet for a Small Planet with Frances Moore Lappé," *The Spirit of Ma'at* 3, no. 1, http://www.netmar. com/~maat/archive/aug3/ twobooks.htm.

Chapter Six

1. Barras, Colin, "Smart amoebas reveal origins of primitive intelligence," *New Scientist*, October 29, 2008, http://www.newscientist.com/article/dn15068-smart-amoebas-reveal-origins-of-primitiveintelligence.html.

2. Lipton, Bruce, *The Biology of Belief: Unleashing the Power of Consciousness, Matter, & Miracles*, (New York: Hay House, 2005), http://nicolevidorlifecoach. blogspot.com/ 2008/10/collective-amoebic-consciousness.html.

3. Dewey, Russell, "Are Animals Conscious," Psych Web, 2007, http://www.psywww.com/intropsych/ ch08_animals/are_animals_conscious.html.

4. Animal Liberation Front, "Animal Sentience," http:// www.animalliberationfront.com/ALFront/FAQs/ AnimalSentience.htm.

Chapter Eight

1. Watts, Alan, *The Book*, (New York: Collier Books, 1966), 6.

2. Dyer, Wayne, *The Power of Intention* (Carlsbad: Hay House, 2004), 82.

Chapter Eleven

1. Hawkins, David R., *Power vs. Force* (Carlsbad: Hay House, 1995), 100–102, 285–286, www.veritaspub. com.

Chapter Thirteen

1. Osho Rajneesh and David Rabe, *Beyond the Frontiers of the Mind* (Blackwell: Osho, 1988), http:// deoxy.org/egofalse.htm.

Chapter Seventeen

1. Chopra, Deepok, *Ageless Body, Timeless Mind: The Quantum Alternative to Growing Old* (New York: Three Rivers:1993), http://quotationsbook.com/ quote/36212/.

2. Phelan, Josho Pat, "Stillness and Contentedness," Chapel Hill Zen Center, 2005, http://www.intrex.net/ chzg/pat34.htm.

Chapter Eighteen

1. Nietzsche, Friedrich http://www.brainyquote.com/ quotes/keywords/whenever.html

Chapter Nineteen

1. Hawkins, David R., *Power vs. Force* (Carlsbad: Hay House, 1995), 20, www.veritaspub.com.

Chapter Twenty Five

1. Katie, Byron, *Loving What Is* (New York, New York: Three Rivers Press, 2002), 1-2.

Chapter Twenty Seven

1. Cain, Fraser, "How Many Galaxies in the Universe," Universe Today, August 7 2009, http://www.universetoday.com/guide-to-space/galaxies/how-many-galaxies-in-the-universe/.

2. Dyer, Wayne, *The Power of Intention* (Carlsbad: Hay House, 2004), 115.

3. Hawkins, David R., *Power vs. Force* (Carlsbad: Hay House, 1995), 285, www.veritaspub.com.

Programs Available from the Author

Speaking Engagements

Weekend Intensives

Seminars

Retreats

Contact Information

To learn more about our books and programs, and for additional contact information, go to our website at:

www.awakentoego.com

Like us on Facebook at <u>Awaken to Ego</u>

Author's email:

dmutchler@beyondtheego.com

About the Author

David Mutchler has earned degrees in education, philosophy, psychology, and social work, with advanced studies in religion.

The painful challenges on his own journey inspired a determined search for the source of and resolution to the troubles most people experience in their lives. In that search, David discovered that the answers lie in the spiritual realm, where ego raises havoc with our spiritual birthrights—joy, love, and peace. As an integrative thinker, he has brought his various studies and life experiences together in a unique perspective that has relevance to individuals, nations, and a globe of diverse peoples.

Two of the trademarks of David's work are his insistence on the simplification of concepts that are typically thought to be both complex and esoteric, and his "how-to" approach to helping people assimilate and apply those concepts to bring more peace into their lives.

David now devotes the majority of his time to writing, speaking, and leading weekend intensives as a spiritual teacher and guide.